LATERAL

LATERAL

Wonderful Answers to Weird Questions

TOM SCOTT & DAVID BODYCOMBE

PUZZLEWRIGHT PRESS and the distinctive Puzzlewright Press logo
are registered trademarks of Sterling Publishing Co., Inc.

© 2024 Tom Scott and David Bodycombe

All rights reserved. No part of this publication may be reproduced,
stored in a retrieval system, or transmitted in any form or by
any means (including electronic, mechanical, photocopying, recording,
or otherwise) without prior written permission from the publisher.

ISBN 978-1-4549-6024-9
ISBN 978-1-4549-6025-6 (e-book)

For information about custom editions,
special sales, and premium purchases, please
contact specialsales@unionsquareandco.com.

Printed in Canada

2 4 6 8 10 9 7 5 3

unionsquareandco.com

Cover design and art by Kaylie Pendleton
Interior design by Christine Heun
Interior grid image by Support Class

CONTENTS

Introduction 6
How to Use This Book 8

Level 1 11
Tips for Solving a Question 12
Warm-Ups 14
Main Questions 17

Level 2 67
How to Host a Question 68
Warm-Ups 70
Main Questions 73

Level 3 125
The Origins of *Lateral* 126
Warm-Ups 128
Main Questions 131

Level 4 177
What Makes a Good Question? 178
Warm-Ups 180
Main Questions 183

Acknowledgments 236
About the Authors 239

INTRODUCTION

My favorite parts of hosting *Lateral* are the lightbulb moments.

Lateral—for those who've picked up this book with no context—is a show about weird questions and wonderful answers. Each question sounds bizarre and impenetrable at first, but, after our panel of three players has spent a few minutes talking through it, eventually they'll be able to work out the strange, surreal, and hopefully satisfying answer. Along the way, they'll be tearing apart the words and the phrasing, making a few deductions and guesses, and no doubt going off on several interesting tangents.

Sometimes the answer will have to be teased out bit by bit, one small deduction at a time. If the players are having trouble, there'll be a few careful hints along the way . . . which is fine! When I'm the one asking a question, I know we'll get there in the end. In the whole history of the show, I think there's only been one or two times when the team has been completely, utterly stumped.

On occasions, there'll be a moment where a player will stumble across a key bit of insight, or they'll have an idea that's sort of connected to the solution. Maybe they'll say something that seems completely irrelevant. Right away, I'll see another player's eyes widen and they'll shout "Oh!" . . . and I'll know that the entire answer has just appeared in their mind: a complete solution, a bolt from the blue, like a cartoon lightbulb just switched on above their head.

Questions on *Lateral*—whether that's on the show or in this book—never rely on just "regular" recall of trivia facts. General knowledge and some pop-culture smarts do help sometimes, but knowing the exact order of monarchs, dates of treaties, and names of capital cities probably won't. The best lightbulb moments are the ones that are completely unexpected: when someone known for science nerdery solves a sports question through a bit of connected knowledge, or when a Gen Z-er suddenly remembers a decades-old pop-culture reference that their grandparents quoted to them when they were young.

In this book are brand-new *Lateral* questions that have never been asked on air, along with the very best of the first 30 episodes of the show. For each, we've included not just the basic question and answer, but also the additional behind-the-scenes notes that don't usually make it to broadcast. You have all the pre-prepared hints and clues, in the order that they're likely to be needed by players. There's also additional background information that helps to fill in the blanks after the question has been answered, as well as some fascinating extra trivia.

As the host, I get to ask about half of the questions on the show. The rest are introduced by the players, with the help of question editor and producer David Bodycombe. I genuinely have no idea what the players are going to ask. This means that I've been able to experience that lightbulb moment myself. When it happens, it feels wonderful. My hope is that as you read through this book, either by yourself or with friends, you get to experience it, too.

—T. S.

HOW TO USE THIS BOOK

With over 100 questions in this book, there's plenty of opportunity for *Lateral* fun, regardless of whether you're challenging yourself or playing as a group with friends, family, or work colleagues.

This book is divided into four difficulty levels. The questions in the easier levels usually require fewer mental leaps to arrive at the right answer. In the harder levels, you may not have as much information given to you, so judicious use of clues and questioning is a must.

At the start of each level are a handful of warm-up questions. Use these as a kind of "palate cleanser" before tackling the main course, and as a way of introducing yourself or anyone unfamiliar with *Lateral* to our unique style.

Each question has four sections: the question itself, five clues (ranked from least to most helpful), the essential solution required, and background notes.

Most of the material is brand-new to this book, but we've also included some of the best questions from the podcast, marked with the label shown at right.

PLAYING BY YOURSELF

If you're flying solo, here's how to play. First, read the main question text to yourself. If no inspiration strikes, read clue 1 and see if that helps. Clues either rule out common incorrect answers or point the way to the right line of inquiry. Keep reading the clues every so often until you think you've solved the question. (Even if you think you've got the right answer, look down the remaining clues just to check.) To see the answer, turn the page.

If you're the competitive sort, you can award yourself points for a correct answer on the following basis:

Clues taken	None	1	2	3	4	5
Points earned	6	5	4	3	2	1

For questions exclusive to this book, Tom has noted the stage at which he got the answer right when he played these questions himself. Can you find the answer as quickly as he did, or even quicker?

If you need some hints on how to solve a *Lateral* question, check out our solving tips on page 12.

PLAYING AS A GROUP

Lateral questions are great icebreakers at home, in the office, when traveling, or wherever people gather. Whoever wants to play host should select a question from the book and read it aloud twice. While the team begins to confer, if they haven't already done so, the host should silently read the solution and background notes to themselves, so that they have the key information needed to answer any queries.

It's up to the host how helpful they want to be. To keep the game moving, the host can—at their discretion—force the team to take the next clue every so often. It could be after an approximate amount of time has passed (e.g., two minutes) or after the team has posed, say, three questions/guesses.

If you want to play competitively, use the same scoring system given above and see what total you can accumulate as a team after, say, six questions.

For additional hosting advice on how to channel your inner Tom Scott, there's a useful guide on playing the "question asker" role on page 68.

LEVEL 1

Tips for Solving a Question

Lateral isn't meant to be a competition, although we've certainly had occasional players who think of it that way! Like a lot of panel shows and parlor games, it's an excuse for a conversation. There's very little entertainment in finding the answers immediately; ideally, there should be plenty of interesting tangents and diversions along the way.

The wonderful thing is that those tangents often help solve the question, too. Questions on *Lateral* are rarely solved by someone recalling a specific fact; instead, it's usually a chain reaction. A joke answer by one player will spark a thought from someone else, which will prompt the third player to tell a story they once heard, which then reminds the first player of something deep in their memory that happens to contain the actual answer. I once opened the discussion on a question by telling what I thought was an irrelevant-but-fun anecdote, an old urban legend. Turns out it wasn't an urban legend; it was precisely the answer to the question.

If you ever feel stuck, with no idea of how to progress, here are a few other hints.

Most *Lateral* questions are based on real events, and often include a date and a place. This is where some general knowledge can come into play. Was there a particular political, social, or technological change around then? If it's the US in 1969, it could be a question about the Moon landings or Woodstock. If it's France in the 18th century, it might well be about the Revolution. You won't need expert knowledge to solve the question, but it can be a useful place to start.

Keep an eye out for sentences where the question writers have been just a little bit vague. If the question says "North

America" or "in the 1980s," ask yourself why no specific country or year is given. Would it be too much of a clue?

Watch out for any unusual words or phrasing. If the question contains "just after landing," for example, the writer might want you to assume that it's about a trip on an airplane. But "landing" can also apply to boats, hovercraft, skydivers, and many other things. Similarly, if a question mentions "turning the wheel" and "applying the brakes," it doesn't necessarily mean it's about someone driving a car.

The questions might include key words that are designed to spark a discussion. See if you can grab on to any of those handholds and start a conversation about them. For example, if the question says "an animal at the zoo," try mentioning a few zoo creatures and see if it leads anywhere.

The most important advice is to talk. If you're on your own, talk out loud to yourself, or have a pen and paper handy to jot down notes and ideas. When playing as a group, don't be afraid to say things that might seem irrelevant or strange. And if someone says something that's irrelevant or strange, don't make fun of them for it. We've lost count of the number of times our guests have found the right answer—or something on the road to it—when they've said something in jest.

—T. S.

Warm-Ups

1

Which town in South Dakota uses the slogan "Where the Battle Wasn't"?

CLUES

- They keep getting confused with a more famous place.
- It's a reference to the American Civil War.

2

A shop has a tray of LEGO bricks on the floor. What is it selling?

CLUES

- It's not a toy shop, and the LEGO bricks are not for sale.
- It also has trays of gravel, stone, and wood bark.

3

Where can you find a triangle-shaped square?

CLUES

- Although triangular, they also have a right angle.
- You might have had one or two of these as a child.

4

In the Afrikaans language, what object is known as a "papier vampir"?

CLUES

- As the name implies, it acts like a vampire.
- Like a vampire, it has two sharp "teeth."

5

Why are Swiss Army Knives red?

CLUES

- It's something related to the conditions in which they are often used.
- If they were white, what could happen to them?

SOLUTIONS

1 Gettysburg.

The town of 1,300 people lies in Potter County, South Dakota. A sign on the edge of this rural outpost reads, "Gettysburg, SD—Where the Battle Wasn't." Similarly, Manhattan in Kansas calls itself "The Little Apple."

2 Shoes.

The shoe shop has a tray of various rough materials, including LEGO bricks, so that customers can try out their new shoes.

The shop is one of the retail locations of the brand Leguano, which sells what it calls "barefoot shoes"—those with a thinner sole that offers more flexibility while still affording some protection against hazards ... such as LEGO bricks.

3 In a geometry set.

A geometry set usually contains a triangle-shaped template called a set square, or square for short.

Also, the rafter's square is a triangular building tool used for measuring and checking for 90-degree angles. The traditional square used by carpenters is usually L-shaped.

Question submitted by Aaron Snider

4 A stapler.

Other Afrikaans words with fun literal translations include "windmeulvliegtuig" (windmill flying plane; i.e., helicopter) and "vlakvark" (flat face pig; i.e., warthog).

5 So you can find them in the snow.

Swiss Army Knives are not a new concept. A Roman version of a pocketknife from the year 200 had an iron blade, spoon, fork, hook (for eating snails), and bottle opener.

Main Questions

QUESTION

When traveling in Iceland, Kristjan noticed that his hotel phone had a special button. When pressed, it might wake you up at an unpredictable time. Rather than being annoyed, people found this very useful. How?

CLUES

- The alarm may not go off at all.
- Hotel staff would trigger the wake-up call.
- However, the staff still couldn't predict when the alarm should happen.
- This is because they were relying on external factors.
- The location of the hotel is highly relevant.

SOLUTION

To wake you up when the northern lights were on display.

NOTES

The phone in each hotel room had a button marked "Northern Lights Wake-Up." Pressing the button would cause the phone to ring if hotel staff noticed that the famous atmospheric phenomenon began during the middle of the night.

■ ■ ■

The northern lights are also known as the aurora borealis, after the Roman goddess of the dawn and the Greek name for the north wind. When a solar storm of charged particles makes its way toward the Earth at speeds of up to 45,000,000 mph, the ions create colors as they meet the oxygen and nitrogen in our upper atmosphere. Green is often seen in areas where auroras commonly occur, but red, pink, blue, purple, and white are also possible with the right conditions. It occurs at the poles because the charged particles are funneled there by the Earth's magnetic field.

The equivalent aurora australis in the southern hemisphere was named by Captain James Cook in the late 17th century while exploring the Antarctic. These southern lights can also be seen in New Zealand, Tasmania, and southern mainland Australia.

In Norse legend, the northern lights were thought to be reflections from the armor of the Valkyries, the female warriors who chose which souls would have the right to enter Valhalla. Some indigenous North Americans believed that the lights were their ancestors' spirits dancing in the sky.

TOM—0 Clues I haven't seen the telephone button in question, but I got this right away. That's possibly because I keep an eye on alerts for aurora happening in Britain.

QUESTION

According to a 2018 survey by the British company YouGov, two-thirds of children aged 6 to 18 could not identify this object. Yet, almost all of them are likely to see a representation of it several times in a typical month. What is it?

CLUES

- They are unlikely to see the item itself.
- The real item has become virtually obsolete.
- However, its shape still has meaning today.
- It's a familiar sight to computer users.
- It's an icon that's often in the top-left corner of the screen.

SOLUTION

A floppy disk.

Question submitted by Ryan Neary

NOTES

Even though it's the icon for the Save command in many pieces of software, 67 percent of the 2,000 children surveyed could not say what a floppy disk was when shown a picture of one.

・・・

From the same YouGov survey:

- 27 percent couldn't identify a typewriter.
- 37 percent couldn't identify a video cassette.
- 71 percent couldn't identify an overhead projector.
- 86 percent couldn't identify a pager.

    Floppy disks were the brainchild of a team of engineers at IBM in the late 1960s. They were originally 8 inches in diameter, before the 5.25- and 3.5-inch versions replaced them. They, in turn, were replaced by the CD-ROM. When Compton's MultiMedia Encyclopedia was launched in 1989, a single CD contained the entire 26-volume Encyclopedia Britannica, Webster's Dictionary, and 15,000 illustrations—a total of 600 megabytes, equal to 1,800 floppy disks at the time.

    In 2019, one in ten of the world's pagers were used by staff of the UK's National Health Service. The government ordered them to be phased out by 2021. The NHS was also one of the last widespread users of fax machines.

    Curiously, the UK road sign for a speed camera represents a Victorian bellows camera from the 1850s, a full century before the speed camera itself came about in 1958. Ironically, the speed camera was invented by racing driver Maurice Gatsonides, who wanted a device to help him improve his lap times.

TOM—4 Clues I was locked in on "rotary phone" until the fourth clue. I suspect this question might be out of date in a few years, as web-based tools constantly save your work after every character you type.

QUESTION

When Yasmin was making some brownies, she was surprised to see a bunch of letters—but she understood what had happened. What was it?

CLUES

- It was letters of the alphabet, not mail letters.
- It is relevant that these were brownies.
- She was toward the end of the production process.
- They were all the same letter.
- They were the letter M.

SOLUTION

The M's from her M&M's had separated.

NOTES

Yasmin had topped her brownies with M&M's. During cooking, the printed letter M's had separated from the chocolate beans, leaving the brownie itself covered with white letters.

■ ■ ■

The name stands for the candy's inventors, Mars and Murrie. They copied Smarties, a British candy, which were eaten by soldiers during the Spanish Civil War. The US Army bought M&M's for World War II soldiers, as they were conveniently mess-free even in tropical climates. Jon Lovitz and John Goodman were the original voices of Red and Green, M&M's advertising mascots or "spokescandies."

Smarties used to have different chocolate centers, such as coffee flavor inside the light-brown shell. Orange flavoring is still added to the shell of the orange Smarties. They did not used to be vegan because the red ones contained cochineal, a dye made from ground beetles. The blue Smartie had to depart in 2007, in anticipation of a new requirement that only natural colorings could be used, but was re-introduced a year later thanks to a colorant made from spirulina seaweed.

Chocolate contains various mind-influencing chemical compounds: endorphins that boost pleasure; the "happiness drug" serotonin; phenylethylamine, a natural antidepressant; and theobromine, which relieves stress. However, dogs can't eat regular chocolate because they are unable to metabolize the theobromine quickly. A fatal dose of chocolate for a human being is around 22 pounds (10 kilograms).

TOM—5 Clues I was a bit baffled as I didn't know it was possible for the letters to do that. Turns out that getting the letters from M&M's to separate and float is a science experiment for kids.

QUESTION

In Australian suburban swimming pools, you will often see a float with a rope tied between it and a nearby tree. Why?

CLUES

- The rope is there "just in case."
- For the same reason, a timber pole leaning against a solid boundary fence is recommended.
- It's helpful to something.
- It's for an ecological reason.
- This problem is unique to Australia.

SOLUTION

To help koalas climb out of the pool.

NOTES

In certain areas of Australia, such as southeast Queensland, koalas roam wild. With their sharp claws, koalas are unable to gain any purchase on the side of a swimming pool if they happen to fall in.

The rope is to allow them to grab on to something rough that will enable them to pull their way out of the pool. People are also advised to install koala-friendly fencing, keep dogs under control, and drive carefully.

■ ■ ■

Koalas aren't bears, but marsupials. They spend up to 18 hours a day asleep, while clinging to their favorite eucalyptus tree. Koalas have a cecum, a long digestive organ, that allows them to break down the eucalyptus leaves they eat, even though they are tough and poisonous. The leaves are low in nutrients, so koalas need to eat up to 2.2 pounds (1 kilo) of them every day. They obtain most of their moisture from eating the leaves, which is why their name means "no drink" in Dharug, an aboriginal language.

Another way of keeping animals out of your pool is to install a pool cover. However, in 2023, a couple from Essex, England, discovered that a herd of 18 water buffaloes had broken into their garden after a farmer's electric fence had failed. Several buffaloes fell into the swimming pool, causing about £25,000 ($32,000) worth of damage to the pool cover. (The animals were rescued unharmed.)

TOM—2 Clues It took me a while to work out exactly which creature and why. I know that little ramps are built into pools to allow frogs, ducklings, chipmunks, and other creatures to escape. Pet owners can also buy "dog escape ramps" in case their pet jumps in but gets too tired to climb out.

QUESTION

Why will you never see a player at many European soccer clubs, such as Lazio and Bayern Munich, or on the NFL's Seattle Seahawks, wearing uniform number 12?

■ ■

CLUES

- It's done out of respect.
- This stunt wouldn't work for a rugby team or a basketball team.
- 12 is chosen because it's one more than 11.
- Who are the first 11?
- The "number 12" is not just one person.

SOLUTION

The "12th man/woman" refers to the team's supporters.

Question submitted by Alessandro

NOTES

The "12th man" is a colloquial term used for the crowd of supporters, cheering on their team. (In the US, the phrase is trademarked by Texas A&M University, where the term originated in 1922.) As a tribute to their fans, many teams have formally retired shirt number 12 over the years:

- Lazio (Serie A, Italy)—retired in 2004
- Bayern Munich (Bundesliga, Germany)—retired since 2002
- PSV Eindhoven (Eredivisie, Netherlands)—retired in 1999
- Fenerbahçe (Süper Lig, Turkey)—retired in 2000
- Seattle Seahawks—retired in 1984

■ ■ ■

In 1872, the first international association football match took place between Scotland and England at a cricket ground in Partick, Glasgow. Teams didn't have shirt numbers because substitutes weren't allowed, and players stayed in their preferred playing position anyway. Numbered shirts made their debut in the English Football League on August 25, 1928, in a match between Arsenal and Sheffield Wednesday. Shirt numbers didn't become a requirement in FIFA competitions until the 1954 World Cup in Switzerland.

Italian club Napoli retired shirt number 10 in honor of Diego Maradona, who led his team to their first-ever Serie A title in 1986–87.

Mohamed Salah, Manuel Neuer, and Javier Pastore have all worn the number 0 on their shirts, because they joined a team on which someone else already had their usual shirt number, or to indicate a new phase in their career.

TOM—2 Clues I figured it had to be something to do with team size. Until then, my main theory was that the shirt had been retired for someone specific and famous, or that it was a number with an unlucky association behind it.

QUESTION

BEST OF

The hypermarket chain Kaufland has an illustration on its packets of spaghetti. At the top, it shows a messy tangle of pasta noodles wrapped around a fork. However, the spaghetti at the bottom becomes perfectly straight. Why?

CLUES

- In the lower part of the picture, the pasta strands don't deviate at all.
- If the picture wasn't so precise, it wouldn't work as designed.
- Some of the strands are thicker than others.
- The illustration has a dual purpose.
- There is a string of numbers underneath.

SOLUTION

The bottom of the illustration doubles as the barcode.

NOTES

Other products have done similarly creative things by disguising the barcode as tree trunks, zebra stripes, a hairbrush, and grass. There is even a product called Bar Code Vodka, which has its barcode pattern on the front of the bottle.

■ ■ ■

The classic black-and-white striped barcodes are Universal Product Codes. Norman Joseph Woodland, the coinventor of the barcode, was inspired by the Morse Code he had learned as a Boy Scout. Writing a series of dots and dashes in the beach sand one day, he used his fingers to extend each symbol into narrow and wide vertical lines. However, the technology requirements weren't practical, and the project was put on the back burner for years.

By the 1970s, laser and computer technology had become smaller and cheaper, making barcode scanning viable. The first product to be officially scanned in a retail shop was a multipack of Wrigley's Juicy Fruit chewing gum in 1974. The cashier, Sharon Buchanan, didn't know that she was going to be part of history when she came into work.

Each "character" in the common UPC-A barcode consists of two black bars. From left to right, it contains the start bars, six digits, middle bars, six digits, and end bars. The 12th number is a check digit to help ensure that the barcode scanner read the lines correctly.

It's estimated that barcodes are scanned 10 billion times per day.

Scan to see an image of the product label.

QUESTION

How did Italian police detectives identify that a barber was selling illegal drugs even though the detectives were sitting some distance away from his shop?

- -

CLUES

- The police knew that drug-selling was happening in the general area.
- They didn't see any drugs being sold or carried overtly.
- The police noticed something unusual.
- Something was "missing" from what they saw.
- The police were observing the barber's clientele.

SOLUTION

Bald, beardless men were going into the barber's shop.

Question submitted by Benjamin Shaw

NOTES

In 2023, police received reports of drug-dealing in an area of Genoa. An investigative unit was dispatched to take up surveillance. One of the police teams noticed that an unusually high number of men were visiting the barbershop even though they were bald and clean-shaven.

When the police organized a raid, they found hashish, cocaine, precision scales, and materials for drug packaging.

■ ■ ■

In the 1850s, doctors encouraged men to grow a beard as a way of warding off illness. They also became fashionable around this time due to soldiers returning from the freezing winters in the Crimean War. In the early 1900s, they were regarded by some as unhygienic and the clean-shaven look became easier to obtain, thanks to King Camp Gillette's new safety razor.

Though the picture is slowly changing, many airlines still don't permit pilots and cabin crew to have beards, even though there is little evidence to suggest they pose a safety hazard. When swimming around the coast of Britain, endurance athlete Sean Conway grew a full beard as a defense mechanism against jellyfish.

The Great Sphinx of Giza originally had a beard, but it fell off at some point. It is now in the basement of the British Museum, but is not on display. Henry VIII, his daughter Elizabeth I, and Russia's Peter the Great all taxed beards.

TOM—STUMPED I got this one confidently wrong. I was certain that the answer was that the customers were leaving with terrible haircuts or unkempt hair.

QUESTION

It's possible for a gardener to produce rainbow roses where the flower head contains four different bright colors. How are they cultivated?

CLUES

- The flower begins as a standard white rose.
- You need a sharp knife for this.
- It uses a scientific principle you may remember from school.
- How could the color effect be transferred to the petals?
- How can different parts of the flower receive different colors?

SOLUTION

By putting different parts of the stem in colored water.

NOTES

In plants, capillary action fights against the effects of gravity so that water can travel through tiny tubes—xylem vessels—to where it's needed.

Here, the stem of a standard white rose is split into four pieces. Each quarter stem is placed into a different color of water. The capillary action "sucks up" the dye into different quarters of the petals, thus giving the rainbow effect.

■ ■ ■

Capillary action occurs when a liquid flows through a narrow tube or space, such as the fibers in a towel, the bristles on a paintbrush, or the holes in a sponge. The effect is also present in candlewicks, drying laundry, and ink markers.

Leonardo da Vinci conducted experiments using liquids in tubes and porous materials, but a formal equation for the effect wasn't developed until Thomas Young did so in the early 19th century.

In the human body, blood flows through networks of tiny capillaries in body tissue, which allow oxygen, nutrients, and waste materials to be exchanged before the blood is pumped back to the heart.

The thorny devil, an Australian lizard, can drink by standing in a puddle of water, thanks to channels in its skin that transport water to the mouth via capillary action.

TOM—0 Clues This is an experiment I remember seeing somewhere, possibly in a science book or as a sidebar in some comic or magazine. If it's any indication of what my childhood interests were, I know I read about this... but I definitely don't remember ever doing it.

Scan to learn more about the process of creating rainbow roses.

QUESTION

In 2018, what did a California branch of McDonald's do to display their support for International Women's Day?

BEST OF

CLUES

- Alas, it didn't involve special offers or paying women employees more.
- The change was visual.
- The change could be seen for miles around.
- A specific part of the restaurant was changed.
- They changed an iconic part of their branding in a clever way.

SOLUTION

They flipped the M of their Golden Arches logo, to make it a W.

NOTES

In 2018, a branch in Lynwood, California, turned their Golden Arches sign upside down, so that it looked like a W instead of an M.

More generally, McDonald's also flipped the letter in their logo/profile picture on their social media accounts.

■ ■ ■

Brothers Richard and Maurice McDonald opened the first McDonald's restaurant in San Bernardino, California, in 1940. It was a BBQ joint for the first eight years of its life before they switched to burgers. They purchased some milkshake machines from Ray Kroc, who was impressed with the concept and started to franchise it elsewhere in 1955. These days, a typical US McDonald's franchise makes $150,000 in profit per year.

The McDonald's sign used to be a single arch, a reference to the large, illuminated architectural arches that the sides of some of their 1950s restaurants featured. The logo didn't become M-shaped until 1962. A branch in Sedona, Arizona, has a turquoise logo, a more tasteful choice given its desert location.

Unusual items that McDonald's have made available in other countries include the Mashed Potato Burger (China), the McNoodles (Austria), red bean pie (Hong Kong), and fried chicken with spaghetti (Philippines). Canada has been spoiled with the Apple Fritter Donut, the McLobster roll, and the famous poutine.

McDonald's has a ski-thru at the Lindvallen ski resort in Sälen, Sweden, and in a video for his YouTube channel, Tom himself tried out a float-thru McBoat collection point on the Elbe River in Hamburg, Germany.

Scan to see the flipped McDonald's logo.

QUESTION

In 2024, why was a sign put up in a branch of the home improvement store Lowe's that read "We can not return any welding helmets purchased on April 7th or April 8th"?

CLUES

- Lowe's is a well-known chain of hardware stores in the US.
- What are welding helmets useful for?
- The items were bought in a hurry.
- Most people had only one use for the helmets.
- Why was April 8, 2024, an important day in the US?

SOLUTION

People had bought them to look at the eclipse.

NOTES

A total solar eclipse happened across mainland US, Mexico, and Canada on April 8, 2024.

Unable to find any official eclipse glasses at the last minute, some people bought welding helmets that had darkened glass on the front that would have a similar effect.

Lowe's was inundated with people returning "faulty" helmets after the event, and put up signs saying that they would not honor returns bought just before the eclipse occurred.

■ ■ ■

Eclipse is derived from the Greek "ekleipsis," meaning "to be abandoned." A total eclipse happens during a "syzygy"—that is, when three celestial bodies (the Sun, Moon, and Earth, in this case) are in alignment.

A total eclipse is a complete fluke of nature in that the Moon happens to be exactly the right size to just cover our view of the Sun. If it happens when the Moon is at the farthest point from Earth in its orbit, a so-called "ring of fire" is seen, making it an annular eclipse instead.

The longest possible period of totality for a fixed point on the Earth is around 7½ minutes. In 2010, passengers on a chartered Airbus managed to experience 9 minutes, 23 seconds. People who travel the world to experience eclipses, the astronomical version of storm chasers, are called umbraphiles.

In a lunar eclipse, the Earth's shadow covers the Moon, causing it to turn blood orange, and the effect can last 1¾ hours.

TOM—0 Clues I didn't see this eclipse myself, but I knew the date it occurred.

QUESTION

Depending on their destination, a pretzel factory would fill some batches of its standard bags so that they were less full. Neither the shops nor the customers complained. In fact, it prevented a lot of annoyance. How?

CLUES

- The bags themselves were the same, regardless of destination.
- That means that something printed on the bags was the same.
- The printed product weight of the pretzels was the same.
- The annoyance would have been a lot of mess.
- They were less "full" of ... what?

SOLUTION

The factory filled the bags with less gas so that they didn't pop when being sent to high-altitude locations.

NOTES

In some parts of the world—such as Chile, Peru, Argentina, or the state of Colorado—people live at altitudes over 10,000 feet.

One effect is that any products that are made at lower altitudes and shipped to higher places can explode. This can happen with any sealed items, such as shampoo, jars of coffee, and bags of potato chips.

For shipments going to these locations, the pretzel-makers put the same number of pretzels into the bags but with less gas, so that they wouldn't pop.

■ ■ ■

For the 2010 FIFA World Cup, the Adidas Jabulani soccer ball had to be designed to perform well at different venues and altitudes, from Durban (at sea level) to Johannesburg (at 5,700 feet). Cans of high-altitude tennis balls are available when playing at elevations above 4,000 feet.

In 2023, a cabin crew member revealed that they use a special technique to combat the significant foam bubbles created when pouring out a Diet Coke on a flight. They put an upside-down cup over an open can, turn the entire thing upside down, then slowly lift the can out of the cup until it's full.

TOM—4 Clues I knew it was "gas" on clue 1, but it took me a long while to figure out the altitude part. Snack companies fill the bags with pure nitrogen as it's readily available and increases the product's shelf life. The extra gas also helps keep the bag from being crushed during transit... provided it doesn't pop.

QUESTION

In 2022, a pickup truck hit a car outside a shopping mall in Roseville, California. Although the driver fled in their vehicle, police investigating the wreck soon arrested the culprit. They just needed a little mental agility, rather than witnesses or CCTV. How?

CLUES

- The method of detection wouldn't have worked if two UK vehicles had collided.
- The culprit didn't drop any ID at the scene.
- However, they did leave some kind of evidence behind.
- The evidence helped track down the truck.
- The "mental agility" involved reading something.

SOLUTION

The truck "imprinted" its license plate number on the car.

NOTES

An imprint of the truck's license plate became "embossed" onto the car it hit. Police simply had to mentally flip the number left to right to identify the correct vehicle. Several similar incidents have occurred in the past, some of which involve the actual torn-off plate being left behind at the crash scene.

■ ■ ■

In many countries that use the Cyrillic alphabet, such as Ukraine, only the letters that have a counterpart in the Latin "A to Z" alphabet appear on vehicle license plates. This is a requirement of the 1969 Vienna Convention on Road Traffic, so that license plates are compatible with administrative systems in other countries.

In 2023, a Dubai resident paid a record-breaking 55 million UAE dirhams ($15 million) for the license plate number "P-7" during an auction. The proceeds went to a food charity. In honor of key workers, strongman Bill Clark improved on his own record in 2020 by tearing 29 metal license plates in one minute.

The first state-issued US license plates were enamel-covered porcelain; the state of Delaware still offers this type for a fee of $110. There are 47 US states that use correctional institutions to manufacture their vehicle tags.

When Joseph Tartaro chose the Californian vanity license plate "NULL," it resulted in $12,049 in traffic fines being sent to him. The computer database used by the California Department of Motor Vehicles defaulted to a value of "Null" if an error or exception occurred.

Scan to read a news article about the collision.

QUESTION

In Quezon City, Philippines, there are four avenues named North, East, West, and Timog (meaning "South"). North Avenue doesn't run north, East Avenue doesn't run east, and so on. Why?

CLUES

- This could potentially happen in any city.
- The four roads can be found in the same area of the city.
- In fact, they are connected to each other.
- Despite the apparent contradiction, the road names are relevant.
- They are almost perpendicular to the direction you'd expect.

SOLUTION

They form the four sides of a square: North Avenue is the north side of the square, and so on.

Question submitted by Allen

NOTES

The four roads enclose a square area of Quezon City. North Avenue is so-called because it forms the northern boundary of that area. However, this means that North Avenue actually runs in a roughly east-west direction. The same thing applies for the other three avenues.

■ ■ ■

When Lord Kitchener's army found Khartoum in ruins in 1898, it is said that he chose to rebuild it in the shape of the Union Jack flag. The eight straight streets leading to the center would offer excellent sight lines to repel any enemy attacks.

Designed by Ildefons Cerdà, the Eixample District in Barcelona, Spain, consists of a repeating pattern of squares with the corners "chamfered." The aim was to give drivers more visibility at intersections, let in more light, and improve airflow.

In northeast Italy, the planned city of Palmanova is a striking design in the shape of a nine-pointed star. A defensive bulwark sits at the tip of each of the points, while radial streets lead to a central piazza.

Walter Burley Griffin's winning plan for a new national Australian capital, namely Canberra, was chosen from 137 different entries. His 1911 design is an intricate set of intersecting circles, triangles, and hexagons. Brasília, Brazil, resembles the shape of an airplane or bird from the air, with housing in the "wings" and civic buildings in the "fuselage."

TOM—STUMPED At first, I confidently thought "Ah, they're named after people!" and skipped ahead to the answer. Nope. Completely wrong. If I'd bothered to read the final clues, I'd have known that.

QUESTION

Roughly 90 percent of the population of the US are right-handed. However, relatedly, there is one road where the vast majority of residents are left-handed. What is it?

BEST OF

CLUES

- As "relatedly" implies, there is a relationship between the first two sentences.
- This street has the exact opposite statistic.
- It's a world-famous road.
- It has been featured on television for years.
- The inhabitants require the help of humans to move.

SOLUTION

Sesame Street.

NOTES

Puppeteers tend to operate the mouth with their dominant hand, which is the right hand for most people. This leaves the other hand (i.e., the left one) to operate the Muppet's active arm.

■ ■ ■

The natural rate of left-handed people is around 10 percent. In Victorian and Edwardian Britain, the rates of left-handedness were artificially forced down to as low as 3 percent by retraining left-handed children. International Left Handers Day is celebrated every August 13.

Etymologically, left-handers get bad press. The word "left" comes from the Old English word "lyft," meaning "weak," and the words "sinister" and "sinistrous" (both meaning "evil") come from the Latin word for the left side.

Left-handers have a disadvantage in sports such as polo and hockey, where everyone must play right-handed for safety reasons. However, they are over-represented in face-to-face sports such as tennis, fencing, and boxing. A "southpaw" boxer leads with their right before taking a shot with their stronger left hand. The term is also used in baseball, where—due to the usual orientation of a stadium—a pitcher's left hand faces the south side. Golfer Phil Mickelson (nicknamed "Lefty") is biologically right-handed, but plays left-handed because he mirrored his father's movements while learning to play.

Most kangaroos are left-handed, but it's a myth that polar bears are—they're ambidextrous.

QUESTION

After Helen finishes work, everything she sees turns slightly purple for a few minutes, even though no one else around her is affected the same way. What is her occupation?

BEST OF

CLUES

- Her vision returns to normal fairly quickly.
- This is not a very common job, but a well-known one.
- Helen's job is in a colorful place.
- Helen is seen in the public eye.
- Her job is in the media.

SOLUTION

She is a television personality (such as a weather forecaster) who works in front of a green screen.

NOTES

Helen works on camera inside a green-screen studio, the kind used by weather forecasters or TV hosts who sit in a virtual, computer-generated set.

If you stare at any plain color for long enough then look elsewhere, the afterimage overcompensates with the complementary or "opposite" color. In this case, the leaf-green color used for green screens is opposite purple on the color wheel.

■ ■ ■

Isaac Newton first arranged colors on a wheel in his 1704 work *Opticks*, though he used seven basic colors compared to the six that modern color wheels use. In his 7th-century text *De natura rerum*, Isidore of Seville thought that there were four colors in the "iris" or rainbow: "From the sky it draws the fiery color, from the waters purple, from the air white, and from the earth it gathers black."

Television cameras that operate in a virtual set need to know where they are in 3D space, so that the computer can matte out the unwanted areas and "paint in" the studio at the correct position and perspective. To achieve this, the camera has a sensor that points to the ceiling, where it can see a pattern of circular barcodes to triangulate its position.

Green and blue are popular choices for the "chroma key" technique because they do not appear in human flesh tones, but any other solid color can work.

QUESTION

At King's Cross railway station in London, an announcement is made at 11 a.m. every September 1 for a train that nobody will board. For whom is the announcement intended?

CLUES

- Not even the staff will board this train.
- The announcement is a bit of fun.
- A crowd of people will come to the station just to hear the announcement.
- When hearing the announcement, some people raise sticks in the air.
- Some people in the station are part of a famous fandom.

SOLUTION

Harry Potter fans.

NOTES

It's a fake announcement for the Hogwarts Express from the Harry Potter universe, going from London King's Cross to Hogsmeade station.

The electronic display says: "Departs from Platform Nine and Three Quarters. A Hogwarts Express service." The station announcement relays the message: "All students are kindly reminded to stick to your ticket, and board the carriage at once."

Fans gather at the station to hear the message, holding their wands aloft. In 2024, the in-person announcement didn't take place, to avoid overcrowding.

■ ■ ■

To cash in on the Harry Potter craze, a luggage trolley has been mounted into the wall of the station as if it is disappearing through an invisible portal. However, it is arguably in the wrong place, being between Platforms 8 and 9. It will be in the correct place if the station's Platform 0 is ever renumbered to 1 (and so on for the others) in the future. In an interview with the BBC in 2001, J. K. Rowling admits that her descriptions of King's Cross don't match with reality because she was mistakenly thinking of Euston station in her mind's eye.

The station is styled as both King's Cross and Kings Cross on various signs and maps. In 2016, Network Rail announced they were dropping the apostrophe to standardize it . . . but it was an April Fool's joke.

In the UK, parliamentary trains (or "ghost trains") are services that run purely to satisfy a legal mandate or minimal service obligation, lest the company lose control of the route. They are badly advertised and run at inconvenient times, with transport geeks often being the only passengers.

TOM—1 Clue At first, "11 a.m." made me wonder about Armistice Day, even though September is the wrong month for that.

QUESTION

Santiago de Compostela Cathedral has been a place of pilgrimage since the Middle Ages. It takes eight people to swing its 80-kilogram (176-pound) incense burner on a 62-meter (68-yard) rope, making it one of the world's largest. Why do locals claim the incense burner was necessary in the past?

BEST OF

CLUES

- Santiago was the end point of a popular pilgrimage route.
- Large groups of pilgrims arrived every day at the church.
- The pilgrimage was made on foot.
- The pilgrims had traveled a long way.
- The pilgrims endured tough conditions with few facilities.

SOLUTION

The incense helped disguise the smell of pilgrims who had traveled to the cathedral.

Question submitted by Manuel Omil

NOTES

The Camino de Santiago ("the Way of St. James") is an ancient 500-mile pilgrimage route. It forms the plot of the 2010 Emilio Estevez-directed movie *The Way*, starring his father, Martin Sheen.

The incense burner is known locally as "Botafumeiro" ("smoke expeller"). It was said to be used to remove the stench (and, supposedly, illnesses) from pilgrims who had walked the many miles to the cathedral. They probably washed where they could, but the opportunity to get themselves and their clothes thoroughly clean was limited.

Each "performance" of the Botafumeiro costs €450 (around $500) to put on. Due to the burner's weight, eight people have to pull the rope, which is changed roughly every 20 years for safety.

■ ■ ■

The scallop shell—a symbol of rebirth and a metaphor for pilgrimage—can be seen in many artworks and buildings along the Camino de Santiago route.

The Al Mashaaer Al Mugaddassah Metro Line operates for only one week a year, to transport pilgrims to Mecca and other holy sites such as Mount Arafat. It runs 24 trains every hour, each one containing 3,000 passengers. It is estimated that building the line has removed the need for 53,000 buses on the roads.

With an attendance of 200 million, the world's largest religious gathering is the Kumbh Mela. Attended by Hindu pilgrims, it takes place at a cycle of four sacred river locations every 12 years.

QUESTION

Architectural domes often resembled a pointed, hemispherical helmet, such as those on the Taj Mahal. Why did this evolve into the famous "onion dome" shape in Russian architecture, as seen on St. Basil's Cathedral?

CLUES

- There was a practical purpose to this.
- What advantage does a roof with a steeper pitch have?
- What is a key difference between India and Russia?
- The design keeps it clear of something.
- What problems does the Russian climate cause?

SOLUTION

It discourages the collection of snow on the dome.

NOTES

The pointy shape of onion domes prevented snow from piling up.

■ ■ ■

Snow is a genuine architectural headache—even on an average-sized domestic roof, one foot of snow adds 10 tons of pressure, the equivalent of four Toyota Land Cruisers.

Completed in the 1st century, the Pantheon in Rome remains the world's largest unreinforced concrete dome. The height from the floor to the oculus (circular opening in the roof) is 142 feet, the same as the diameter of the interior. As the name "Pantheon" implies, it was built as a temple to all gods.

The world's largest dome is found at the 55,000-seat Singapore National Stadium. It is 1,020 feet (312 meters) in diameter, with a retractable roof that can be opened or closed for rugby, association football, athletics, and cricket.

London's O2 venue, originally called the Millennium Dome, takes inspiration from units of time, after its location near to the Greenwich prime meridian. It is 365 meters in diameter, 52 meters high, and is supported by 12 steel masts—representing the number of days, weeks, and months in a year.

In New Delhi, India, the roof of the Lotus Temple—a Baha'i house of worship—is made from 27 marble-covered "petals" to form a nine-sided flower. The shell-shaped structures of the Sydney Opera House are meant to evoke the sails of ships sailing by.

TOM—4 Clues The second clue gave me "snow," but I thought it was less about keeping the roof clear and more about stopping big clumps of snow from falling on people. An onion-shaped roof wouldn't help with that!

QUESTION

In the reception area of the Australian Red Cross, there is a set of eight electronic displays that look like thermometers, which are regularly updated. The displays are labeled with two or three symbols from a selection of five. What motivation do they provide?

BEST OF

CLUES

- The "thermometers" go up and down, but not due to heat.
- The fact that there are eight signs is relevant.
- Three of the five symbols are letters.
- The signs might prompt people to be altruistic.
- What would the Red Cross organization want people to do?

SOLUTION

For people to give blood.

NOTES

The signs show the current stock levels at the blood bank for each of the eight types of blood (O+, O-, A+, A-, B+, B-, AB+, AB-).

■ ■ ■

Most men have 10–12 pints of blood in their body, while women have 9–10. The liquid plasma contains three cell types: red blood cells that transport oxygen via hemoglobin; white blood cells that fight off infections; and platelets that help the blood to clot after an injury.

Sir Christopher Wren (famous for building St. Paul's Cathedral in London) was an early experimenter in blood transfusion, and Richard Lower achieved a transfusion between animals in 1666. James Blundell performed human transfusions from 1818, but they remained risky operations until Karl Landsteiner discovered the compatibility rules for blood groups in 1901.

The four main blood groups (O, A, B, and AB), together with Rhesus positive or negative, indicate what antigens—antibody generators—you have. Someone in the AB+ group (meaning they have the A, B, and Rhesus D antigen in their blood) can receive any blood type; whereas O- is the universal donor. Thirty-six percent of people have O+, the most common type, while fewer than one percent have AB-, the rarest type.

In Japan, people judge romantic compatibility based on each other's blood group, similar to zodiac signs. In the UK, theatrical stage blood is known as Kensington Gore, a pun on a London street name. A traditional coq au vin is thickened with rooster blood mixed with vinegar to prevent clotting, while black pudding contains pig blood.

Scan for a photo of the Australian Red Cross lobby display

QUESTION

It's often seen next to a spider, mainly green in color and marked with lines and spots. At full size, it has six pairs of jaws and six legs. What is it?

CLUES

- It's also often seen next to a bridge.
- It's not an insect.
- It's not even alive.
- It's not something that's found in many houses, unless you have a lot of space.
- The green comes from colored felt.

SOLUTION

A pool or snooker table.

NOTES

A full-size pool or snooker table has six legs for support, and six pairs of cushioned "jaws" that are angled to make it easier to sink the balls in the pockets.

The lines and spots are used to position the balls in the correct places. One of the additional supports for the cue (known as "rests" in snooker and "bridges" in pool), used for making awkward shots, is called a "spider."

■ ■ ■

Snooker was a development of billiards by British army officers serving in India. In 1875, they added colors to the existing ivory balls to make the game more interesting. The name may derive from old military slang for a new cadet.

The green baize used to cover a snooker table provides good color contrast, and it's perhaps an allusion to outdoor lawn games—the colored balls in snooker are similar to those in croquet. Snooker enjoyed a boon when the BBC began color broadcasting, although that caused issues for the commentators. "Whispering" Ted Lowe once said, "For those of you watching in black and white, the pink is next to the green."

Developed in the 1930s, bar billiards is a table game that is played from one end and so uses much less floor space. The targets are holes in the middle of the table, and mushroom-shaped skittles end your turn or even wipe out your score to zero.

The "chalk" used by the players of cue sports to improve friction is a mixture of silica and corundum crushed together.

TOM—0 Clues Got it right away! This will be more difficult for people outside the UK, where the smaller pool tables they'll find in a bar probably won't have a "spider."

QUESTION

Shelley took a selfie at Toronto Airport at 1 p.m. She then visited Paris, Vienna, Seville, Copenhagen, London, Zurich, Dublin, Brussels, and Lisbon, arriving back at Toronto Airport by 8 p.m. that day. How?

CLUES

- It has nothing to do with embassies.
- Her trip took seven hours in total.
- She genuinely visited all the places listed.
- Most people could do this feat quite easily if they wanted to.
- She didn't use any air travel.

SOLUTION

She visited namesakes of the famous cities. (They are all places in Ontario, Canada.)

NOTES

She simply rented a car and drove to various places in Ontario, which are all named after famous world cities. The trip is 370 miles (600 kilometers) long and takes seven hours on a good day.

Ontario also has settlements called Athens, Florence, Glasgow, Palermo, Perth, Verona, and Warsaw.

■ ■ ■

It is possible to sail between London and the abandoned settlement of Paris in a few minutes because they lie on opposite sides of St. Stanislas Bay on the island nation of Kiribati.

Given the understandable influence of the Pilgrim Fathers, New England contains numerous towns and cities named after British cities, including London, Connecticut; Manchester, New Hampshire; and Cambridge, Massachusetts.

If you're going to Kingston in the county of Surrey, be sure you're headed to the right one. The capital of Jamaica fits this description, as did a town in southwest London at one time (it's now in Greater London, strictly). Jamaica's other two counties—Cornwall and Middlesex—are also named after English counterparts.

There are over 1,700 places named San José (or San Jose) after Joseph, the husband of the Virgin Mary in Christian tradition. San Antonio runs a close second place.

The 1984 Wim Wenders film *Paris, Texas* is named after a real city that features a 65-foot replica of the Eiffel Tower with a cowboy hat on the top of it.

TOM—0 Clues I knew this one right away, but then, I've been to a lot of strange places!

QUESTION

In 1966, Yoko Ono devised a chess set called "Play It by Trust." It uses 32 standard chess pieces and an 8×8 square board. What was unusual about it?

BEST OF

CLUES

- It is possible to begin a normal game of chess using this artwork.

- Both players had a full complement of the usual pieces (i.e., eight pawns and eight major pieces).

- The key word in the title is "Trust."

- The game becomes difficult to play after a few moves.

- While the pieces are standard, there is something about them that will be confusing.

SOLUTION

All the pieces are the same color—white.

NOTES

Both players start with a full complement of 16 white chess pieces. While it's possible to start a game in the usual manner, it becomes harder to remember which piece belongs to which player.

The artwork, created in 1966, is symbolic of the futility of war.

■ ■ ■

By 1958, Alex Bernstein had written a program that could play chess, but it could be beaten by novice players. Chess is a difficult game for computers to model because the number of games increases rapidly. After each player has taken just two moves, there are 197,281 possible board positions. Named after a US mathematician, the Shannon Number is a conservative estimate for how many chess games exist, given that the typical length of a game is 40 moves; that number is 10^{120} (or, to put it another way, a 1 followed by 120 zeroes).

A "zugzwang" is a situation in chess where a player would rather not make a move because it will weaken their position; however, they are forced to do so because it is their turn. Another German term, "zwischenzug," refers to a nasty surprise that happens when your opponent replies with a threatening move you weren't expecting. "Checkmate" comes from the Persian "shah mat," meaning "the king is dead."

When commentators annotate chess games, they can add punctuation after a move (e.g., e4!) to offer an opinion on its strength: "!" is good, "!!" is brilliant, and "?" and "??" are increasing degrees of error. The notation "!?" is an interesting move that might not be the best, and "?!" signals that the move might be dubious.

Scan to see an image of the artwork.

QUESTION

An astronaut on the International Space Station needed a ratcheting socket wrench that wasn't on board. However, he managed to have exactly what he needed a short time later without cannibalizing any parts of the ISS. How?

CLUES

- The next rocket was not due for four months.
- Despite its name, it was a relatively basic tool.
- The astronaut had the tool needed within a few hours.
- It wasn't sent physically.
- They have more facilities on the ISS than you might think.

SOLUTION

The astronaut made one with a 3D printer.

NOTES

The company Made in Space, Inc. (now Redwire Space, Inc.) designed and installed a 3D printer on the ISS. Twenty objects had been printed in space as part of a test.

In 2014, when they overheard ISS commander Barry Wilmore talking about a wrench they needed, the company decided to make a 3D model for one. This file was sent to NASA, which transmitted it to the ISS. The 3D printer then "manufactured" the wrench. This was the first time a 3D object had been made for an astronaut at their request.

■ ■ ■

Since the first working 3D printer was announced by Hideo Kodama in 1981, they have been used to manufacture things at scales ranging from a 39-foot (12-meter) boat to a sculpture of a drum that's just 47 microns across—about the width of a human hair.

In 2013, the European Space Agency announced plans to use lunar soil to 3D-print a base near the south pole of the Moon. Structures that have already been manufactured using a 3D printer include a bridge in China (2020), a laboratory in Dubai (2021), and a villa in the UAE (2023).

Garth Minette released a design for a 3D printer that could be largely manufactured using . . . a 3D printer. The RepRap Snappy 1.1c model requires 107 pieces, 85 of which can be 3D printed.

In medicine, 3D printing has been used to create replacement jaws, ribs, and even bionic ears.

TOM—4 Clues I got this on "wasn't sent physically," but it took me a while to believe that someone had successfully made a 3D printer that works in microgravity.

QUESTION

BEST OF

You sit back in your chair, sip your drink, and think "I'm having a great time here in Vegas." But then you start to worry. Some people seem to be getting very lucky in your craps game. How could you quickly and easily tell whether the dice being used were "loaded"?

CLUES

- You can cheat at craps by "shaping" the dice, but we're talking about loaded dice.
- Loaded dice have one side that is more likely to come up than the other.
- That's because loaded dice have one side that is heavier than the others.
- How could you test for one side being heavier?
- Is there something you might have in your hand that could help you?

SOLUTION

Place the dice in your drink and watch how they float.

NOTES

If you put the dice in your drink and the same side keeps floating to the top, it is likely that the dice aren't fair.

There are some more difficult ways of detecting loaded dice. For example, you can hold one lightly at the corners, between your index finger and thumb, and spin it using the other hand. Casinos check for loaded dice with a machine that uses the same principle. The device clamps the die at the points between two opposite corners, and the die will twist to the same position if it is unbalanced.

■ ■ ■

Casino dice are made from clear cellulose acetate to make it difficult to hide any weights inside. Sometimes cheaters will drill out the "spots" of the dice, fill them with a dense metal, and cover them over.

Another popular method of cheating in craps involves swapping out the dice for a different pair that contains the number "6" on two opposite sides. This raises the chance of winning from 49 percent to 58 percent. One of the simplest cheats is "dice control"—throwing the dice in particular ways so that they land on the numbers you want more often than not.

In 2009, Patricia Demauro played a single turn of craps for 4 hours and 18 minutes, ending with a "7" on her 154th roll. The probability of this happening is 5.6 billion to 1, and it earned Demauro an estimated $180,000.

QUESTION

In 1988, white T-shirts with a single black stripe diagonally across them began to be sold in Italian markets. Why?

BEST OF

CLUES

- This concept could be useful in many other countries, too.
- The direction of the diagonal stripe is important.
- The black line was about two inches wide.
- The T-shirts were designed due to a change in the law.
- People were trying to avoid something.

SOLUTION

To make it look like a car's driver is wearing a seat belt.

NOTES

Italy changed the law in 1988 so that seat belts became compulsory. The T-shirt's broad, black stripe—from the shoulder to the opposite waist—looked like a seat belt, giving the impression that the driver was complying with the new regulations.

■ ■ ■

The first "seat belt" was invented before the car. In 1885, Edward J. Claghorn was awarded a patent for a kind of safety harness that would keep passengers safe when riding on the horse-drawn carriages of New York City.

The modern three-point seat belt was invented by Nils Bohlin, a Swedish engineer working at Volvo, in 1959. Seat belt design has been improved over time with features such as the "pretensioner" (which tightens the belt when the car is in a crash) and the "load limiter" (which reduces the maximum pressure on the chest).

According to the US NHTSA (National Highway Traffic Safety Administration), 91.9 percent of people used seat belts in 2023. They claim that 14,955 lives were saved by seat belts in 2017 (over 40 a day), but 2,549 more could have been saved if everyone buckled up. All 50 US states have a seat belt law for adults except for New Hampshire.

In the UK, you don't have to wear a seat belt if you're investigating a problem with a vehicle that requires the vehicle to be in motion, are a licensed taxi driver, or are making deliveries that are less than 55 yards (50 meters) apart.

Scan to see the T-shirt (among other law-circumventing innovations).

How to Host a Question.

Lateral is designed as a team game with one person asking a question to the others. So, if you're ready to step into my shoes as host of your own game, here are a few tips to get you started.

First up: read the question out loud twice. Originally, on the podcast, we repeated the question in case listeners were distracted for a moment. That repetition turned out to give the players, and the audience, some important thinking time: a few seconds to work out what the question is asking for, and what possible avenues there are to solve it.

Once you've asked the question, stay quiet. There will be a few seconds of awkward silence. You'll be really tempted to immediately offer help, but it's far better for one of the players to try and fill that gap. At most, prompt with "What do you think?" or something similar. Hopefully, one of them will lead the conversation.

If someone in the group gasps that they immediately know the answer, through either existing knowledge or an immediate deduction, ask them to sit back and let the others have a shot. If they're right, they can confirm the solution later; if it transpires that they're wrong, they can jump back in.

If no one's anywhere close to the answer after a minute or two, it's time to get to work. Give out just enough hints at a steady speed so that the players can progress without feeling that they're being led directly to the answer. As with any group discussion, you may have to do a bit of moderation: if there's one person who's staying very quiet, take note if their eyebrows suddenly raise so that you can direct the conversation to them.

Don't feel obliged to answer every question that the players ask aloud. Some groups of players can fall into what I call

"Twenty Questions" mode. Instead of discussing things among themselves (Fun! Entertaining! Great for the audience!), they'll just end up firing off a lot of short, simple questions. Asking "Is it large? Is it red? Is it upside down?" tends to stop the discussion in its tracks. To redirect them back onto a better path, a well-timed hint and an open-ended question will get them talking among themselves, rather than interrogating the questioner.

If players are on the right track, confirm it so that they don't expend pointless energy coming up with further possibilities. For a team completely on the wrong path... let them go along that wrong path just for a little while before you direct them back. If they're having fun talking about it, or the stories they're coming up with are interesting, there's no harm in the occasional detour.

Is the team aimlessly lost and not having fun? Read the next clue out loud and then stay quiet, just like at the start of the question, to give them time to digest it. There's an art to timing this sort of thing, and it's one I had to learn during the first few episodes I recorded. Don't expect to get it spot-on right away.

If you're lucky, someone may have one of those lightbulb moments. When a player gets close enough to the answer, you can give them the final nudge they need to get over the finish line. As the final piece of the jigsaw falls into place, let them enjoy their "punch the air" moment. As we've said on *Lateral* since Episode 1, we have no prizes to offer other than bragging rights.

—T. S.

Warm-Ups

1

A Reddit user was amused to find that their athletic shorts were made in a highly appropriate country. Which one?

CLUES

- This is a famous name in sportswear.
- It's a brand more associated with sneakers.

2

What can you add to "one" to make it disappear?

CLUES

- It's not –1. Think of the word "one" rather than the number.
- You need to add a single letter.

3

In a standard Helvetica font, which two consecutive letters of the alphabet are mirror images of each other?

CLUES

- We are using the standard ABC alphabet.
- It may help to think about writing like a small child.

4

What can have a blood pressure of 300 over 180?

CLUES

- What might need to pump blood a long way?
- Specifically, in an upward direction.

5

What movie did James Cameron successfully pitch by drawing the letter "S," then two vertical lines?

CLUES

- Before adding the "S," he wrote the title of the original film in the franchise.
- This sequel's title is thematic to the franchise's general plot progression.

SOLUTIONS

1 Jordan.

Their Air Jordan shorts were made in Jordan, the Arab country in western Asia.

2 G—and then it's GONE.

3 Lowercase "p" and "q."

The phrase "mind your p's and q's" possibly comes from the days of choosing letter blocks of type when compiling a page for the printing press. This was especially tricky, as the letters were assembled back to front so that they would look correct when printed on the paper.

4 A giraffe.

Given that 180 over 120 is classified in humans as a hypertensive crisis, a BP of 300 over 180 is really high. However, it's only that high in the giraffe's heart—in the head, it's about the same as a human.

5 *Aliens*.

James Cameron followed the success of *Terminator* by pitching a sequel to Ridley Scott's 1979 sci-fi thriller *Alien*.

He wrote ALIENS, then turned it into ALIEN$, as a way of emphasizing the likely commercial success. (It grossed around $180 million.)

Cameron said: "I wrote ALIEN in large block letters. And I put an S on the end. I said, 'I want to call it ALIENS because we're not dealing with one. But here's what it's going to translate to . . .' And then I drew the two lines through it to make it a dollar sign. And that was my pitch."

Question submitted by Josh Halbur

Main Questions

QUESTION

A 2011 advertisement on Spanish television showed three friends looking at an illuminated sign. They wondered aloud what the number 12,939 meant. What was it advertising?

CLUES

- The number does not represent a statistic or a code.
- The tail of the number 9 was a simple vertical line.
- The lights were illuminated spheres.
- 12,939 is the only number that would work for this ad.
- It's a matter of perspective.

SOLUTION

Pepsi.

Question submitted by Geoffrey Klassen

NOTES

The billboard is made from a matrix of lights. The friends look at the sign, not realizing that they are seeing it from the back. The final shot pulls back from the other side of the billboard to reveal that they are looking at the letters of the word PEPSI.

■ ■ ■

"Brad's Drink" was created in 1893 by the North Carolina pharmacist Caleb Bradham. Believing that the drink aided the digestive system, he changed the name five years later to "Pepsi-Cola," a reference to dyspepsia and pepsin. One ad claimed it was "Healthful and invigorating. Cures nervousness, relieves exhaustion, promotes digestion."

In 1989, PepsiCo, Inc. became the owner of the sixth-largest submarine fleet in the world. The Soviet Union offered 17 submarines (plus a cruiser, frigate, and destroyer) as payment for cola syrup. The vessels were obsolete and only worth their scrap value.

The Netflix docuseries *Pepsi, Where's My Jet?* chronicles the real story of student John Leonard, who earned seven million points in a promotion that—according to a TV ad—would entitle him to an AV-8B Harrier II jet (a prize worth over $60 million in today's money).

In the Ricky Gervais film *The Invention of Lying*, a brutally honest ad bears the slogan "Pepsi—When they don't have Coke." *Modern Family* star Sofía Vergara appeared in a Pepsi ad when she was 17.

TOM—0 Clues I thought of calculator spelling immediately. I turned the numbers upside down in my head and got "bebzi." That was close enough to make the connection.

QUESTION

Sarah is at a party supply store. She can buy a particular item in packs of even numbers, such as 6, 10, or 24. However, one pack contains 13 of this item. What is it, and why 13?

CLUES

- There are no other odd-numbered packs.
- The item comes in various colors, shapes, and sizes.
- What things might you need to buy for a party?
- In the pack of 13, there are nine different shapes.
- The other packs are more versatile, but the pack of 13 items can only be used at a certain kind of party.

SOLUTION

Candles that spell "HAPPY BIRTHDAY."

Question submitted by Sarah

NOTES

The 13-pack was a set of novelty "letter" candles spelling out the phrase "HAPPY BIRTHDAY." The other packs of candles were of the standard rod-shaped variety.

■ ■ ■

The tradition of cake candles was popularized in Germany. At Kinderfest, children would be given cakes that had a single candle. In 1746, Count Ludwig Von Zinzendorf had a birthday party where the cake had one candle for each year of his birth.

Candles feature in many Guinness World Records. The record for the most lit candles on a cake (72,585) was set in honor of a New York meditation teacher. Blowtorches were used for ignition. In 2023, Diego Crescenzi took 40.18 seconds to extinguish 30 candles using a trial bike (this was done by balancing on the back wheel while hopping from candle to candle, snuffing out flames with the front wheel), while the record for "most candles extinguished by a whip in one minute" stands at 102.

The term for a candle maker is "chandler," related to chandelier, the hanging roof light fitting. Candlepower is the former name of the candela, the SI unit of luminous intensity; that is, the amount of light emitted in a particular angular direction.

Trick candles work thanks to magnesium impregnated into the wick. When the flame is blown out, the lower ignition point of the magnesium makes the vapor re-ignite.

TOM—4 Clues The "nine different shapes" gave it away for me, and I started spelling out "HAPPY BIRTHDAY" in my head. I was thinking of balloons rather than candles at first.

QUESTION

"Police _____ _____ Was Accidental"—which two words have been removed from this newspaper headline from a 1993 film?

BEST OF

CLUES

- The headline appears in a mocked-up edition of the *San Francisco Chronicle*.
- The newspaper is an integral part of the plot.
- The redacted words inspired the film's main character.
- It's a film starring Robin Williams.
- The newspaper report relates to an arson.

SOLUTION
"Doubt Fire."

NOTES
The full headline reads "Police Doubt Fire Was Accidental." In the film *Mrs. Doubtfire*, Robin Williams's character devises his alter ego's name when reading this headline.

■ ■ ■

Founded in 1915, the Burbank-based company Earl Hays Press makes fake money, IDs, magazine covers, food packaging, and countless other props for Hollywood. Owner Ralph Hernandez Sr. recounts an occasion when a row of cars with fake Earl Hays license plates were parked on Hollywood Boulevard, saying: "A cop came along and thought he'd hit the jackpot. He issued a ticket to every one." The company maintains antique printing presses and paper-cutting machines to ensure authenticity.

As *Escape This Podcast* cohost Dani Siller correctly pointed out on *Lateral*, the *Mrs. Doubtfire* newspaper appears on the pilot episode of *Charmed*. Identical copies of another prop newspaper have appeared on numerous films and TV series, including *No Country for Old Men*, *Back to the Future*, *Desperate Housewives*, and *Modern Family*.

This type of plot point—a character looking at something in the room to come up with a name quickly—is called "Line-of-Sight Alias" on the TV Tropes website. Other famous instances include (spoiler alert) the legend of Keyser Söze in *The Usual Suspects* and Jan Brady's fake boyfriend George Glass in *The Brady Bunch*.

The Robin Williams film is based on the novel *Madame Doubtfire* (*Alias Madame Doubtfire* in the US) by British author Anne Fine. She took the name from the owner of a bric-a-brac shop.

QUESTION

A British road sign reads:

Finchley	2
M1	5
Brent Cross	5
Watford	15

How did an anonymous prankster add six identical things to raise a smile?

CLUES

- They were small, white things.
- They were pieces of electrical tape.
- The pieces of tape were paired together in different ways.
- They formed basic symbols.
- The symbols enabled the numbers to make sense in a new way.

SOLUTION

They made it look like a valid mathematical equation.

NOTES

They added pieces of white electrical tape so that the numbers formed the equation 2×5+5=15.

■ ■ ■

In 1987, students at Caltech (the California Institute of Technology) used hundreds of dollars' worth of white and black plastic to adapt the famous HOLLYWOOD sign so that it read CALTECH instead. Other pranks pulled by students in Caltech's long history include plastering over an undergraduate's door so that it effectively disappeared, and assembling a fully working Ford Model T in a dorm room.

In a famous 2004 prank, a squad of 20 Yale students managed to arrange a pile of 1,600 red-and-white placards before the annual football game with Harvard. By rearranging the cards into a specific order, the crowd inadvertently spelled out the message "WE SUCK" (instead of the intended "GO HARVARD").

The French-born artist Clet Abraham is known for altering city road signs to give them a new, witty meaning. For example, an arrow on a One Way sign may have a heart added to evoke the spirit of Cupid, or a sumo wrestler might be drawn on a No Entry sign as if they are struggling to carry the central white bar.

Some signs don't need any alteration to be amusing. Real-life examples include a school advertising their "Leteracy Night" (sic) and a *Titanic* exhibit that was "closed due to water damage."

TOM—2 Clues I figured this one out backward. I got the equation immediately, but the clues had to give me "white electrical tape."

Scan to see a photo of the modified sign.

QUESTION

In a corridor, a call button printed with an "up arrow" is on a long, blank wall. The corresponding elevator door is at least 30 feet away. Why is the button positioned there?

CLUES

- Other than being on a blank wall, there is nothing unusual about the call button itself.
- There is a normal set of call buttons next to the elevator, too.
- The corridor has a limited number of places where you can enter.
- Putting it another way, the button is about 20 paces from the elevator.
- Most people would encounter the button before the elevator door.

SOLUTION

So that the elevator arrives when you reach the door.

NOTES

Most people enter the long corridor from the same direction. Walking toward the elevators, they will see the button on the wall first. They can then press the button to call the elevator and keep walking forward. The idea is that the elevator will arrive at approximately the same time as the person arrives at the door.

If they don't notice—or don't understand—the first button, a regular button is positioned next to the elevator door, too.

■ ■ ■

Elisha Otis demonstrated his elevator design in 1854 at the World's Trade Fair in New York. He stood on a raised platform and cut the supporting cable to show that the incorporated safety device would prevent the elevator from falling.

Before the innovation of elevators, the top floor of a building was regarded as a place where poor people lived. Early elevators were called "rising rooms" and sometimes had upholstered benches for passengers to take the weight off their feet while they were slowly taken to their destination.

The elevator to the 163rd floor of the Burj Khalifa skyscraper in Dubai takes passengers on a journey of over a third of a mile. This is the technical limit for standard elevators; otherwise, the steel cables start to take too much strain due to their own weight.

TOM—0 Clues I got this one quickly. I once lived in a building with a slow elevator, and considered trying to rig some sort of remote-control system so I could call the elevator in advance. I figured it was probably best not to mess about with something like that, though.

QUESTION

Every so often, hermit crabs line up in a very particular way. What benefit do they gain by doing so?

- -

CLUES

- They line up in a sequence.
- The sequence is smallest to largest.
- The benefit is mutual to all the crabs.
- What are hermit crabs famous for?
- You could say it's a form of recycling.

SOLUTION

To swap shells to the next crab down the line.

NOTES

The crabs form a kind of conga line, where the largest crab gets into their new, larger home, leaving an empty shell. The next crab in line takes that leftover shell, leaving an empty shell themselves. This goes down the line until they have all moved up one position in the chain.

Suitable shells are few and far between, so this method makes it easy for all the crabs to move to new premises most efficiently.

■ ■ ■

Both halves of a hermit crab's name are misnomers: They're known to circulate in groups of up to 100, and they can't be called true crabs because they don't have a full-body, hard exoskeleton. This is why they borrow discarded shells from other animals to protect their soft tail. They have been known to mistake plastic bottle caps for shells.

Horseshoe crabs are often called "living fossils" because they predate dinosaurs. Their bright-blue blood is rich in copper (like Spock's green blood in *Star Trek*) and can be used to detect bacteria on medical instruments.

The crab is associated with the astrological sign Cancer (which is the Latin word for "crab"); the disease shares the same name because Greek physicians noted that a pattern of crab-like veins often formed in malignant tumors.

TOM—0 Clues I remembered this one from a nature documentary a while back.

QUESTION

American comedian Steve Harvey sent a television to his sixth-grade teacher for Christmas each year until she died. Why?

BEST OF

CLUES

- Her death is not relevant to the question.
- She didn't want, or need, another television every year.
- Though it seems like a nice gesture, Harvey was being passive-aggressive.
- He was getting revenge against the teacher.
- What might a teacher say that could emotionally disappoint a child?

SOLUTION

The teacher thought that Harvey would never be a television star.

NOTES

Harvey had a stutter at school. When he wrote as part of a school assignment that he wanted to be on television, his teacher thought it was ridiculous. So much so that she phoned his parents to say that Harvey had been a "smart aleck." Luckily, Harvey's father supported his goals, and the rest is history.

■ ■ ■

Broderick Stephen Harvey Sr. was born in Welch, West Virginia, in 1957. Prior to showbiz, he had been an insurance salesman, carpet cleaner, mailman, and boxer. In the late 1980s, after his first divorce, he lived in a 1976 Ford Tempo car and showered at gas stations and swimming pools. In 2000, he costarred in Spike Lee's famous stand-up comedy film *The Original Kings of Comedy*.

Harvey took over as host of *Family Feud* in 2010. Some of the more famous answers he's received from contestants during his tenure include: "Name a number most men exaggerate" (Contestant: "A hundred"), "Name something that's hard to do with your eyes open" (Contestant: "Read"), and "Name something that follows the word 'pork'" (Contestant: "Upine").

Steve Harvey had a difficult moment as host of Miss Universe 2015. He announced that Miss Colombia had won, when in fact Miss Philippines, Pia Wurtzbach, was the correct winner. Harvey said that he was told to read the name on his cue card rather than the one on the teleprompter.

QUESTION

In January 2024, Joe Biden won the Democratic Party's New Hampshire primary election. Why was this particularly remarkable?

CLUES

- This Joe Biden was indeed the 46th president, not someone else with the same name.
- An organizational disagreement before this primary made matters more complex.
- US elections have a special rule, which was needed in this case.
- His supporters were able to make their voices heard despite an obvious issue.
- Biden's team had not filled out some paperwork.

SOLUTION

He wasn't listed on the ballot.

NOTES

Joe Biden wanted to let South Carolina have the privilege of running its primary first, in part because its demographics were more closely aligned with the Democratic Party as a whole (and probably in part because he finished fifth in 2020's New Hampshire primary). Expecting to get his way, Joe Biden didn't campaign or register in New Hampshire. Undeterred, New Hampshire went ahead with the elections, as its state law says that it must be first.

New Hampshire primaries allow write-in candidates, where voters can write the name of their preferred choice even if they are not listed on the ballot. After an effective write-in campaign, 79,455 voters put down Biden's name, taking 63.9 percent of the total vote.

The New Hampshire primary decides how the state's (relatively small) number of delegates are allocated to the Democratic and Republican nominating conventions.

■ ■ ■

In 1845, Congress decreed that the US presidential election should happen in November, because the harvest would be complete, and the weather and daylight hours would still be conducive to voting.

In the 1872 election, Ulysses S. Grant found himself in an unusual position when his opponent was a corpse. Newspaper editor Horace Greeley (who coined the phrase "Go west, young man") died before the Electoral College met. Most of the votes previously pledged to Greeley were redirected to minor candidates.

Since anybody's name can be entered for write-in votes, some electors scribble down "Nobody" or a comical suggestion for their preferred candidate. Common unwitting recipients of votes include Mickey Mouse, Jesus Christ, and Willie Nelson.

TOM—5 Clues I got stuck on all sorts of ideas about primary technicalities and weird election rules, and couldn't figure out the much more simple answer.

QUESTION

Printed on the side of an 11-pound box of supplies, there is a stick man with arms aloft. Above him are about 30 smaller shapes, all similar to each other. Also, a message reads "WARNING—DO NOT OPEN OUTSIDE." What is the hazard?

CLUES

- The hazard would only be a problem when outdoors.
- The man appears distressed. He has an open box beside him.
- A much smaller box probably wouldn't need this warning.
- The man is worried about the 30-or-so things above him.
- The scene is somewhat reminiscent of a Hitchcock film.

SOLUTION

A flock of birds.

NOTES

The box contains mealworms. A large box of worms would attract the attention of many common wild birds, including robins, sparrows, starlings, and thrushes. The illustration shows a man next to an opened box, being hassled by a flock of birds as they try to get to the tasty worms.

The clue about the film is referring to Alfred Hitchcock's *The Birds* (1963), in which Rod Taylor and Tippi Hedren's characters are subjected to a series of avian attacks. In 1961, a real-life assault of aggressive shearwater birds in California, possibly triggered by poisoned anchovies, was studied by Hitchcock in preparation for the film.

■ ■ ■

Mealworms aren't worms, but the larva stage of the darkling beetle (*Tenebrio molitor*). Native to Africa, they live in moist, dark conditions such as under logs and in rotten vegetation, and are a common sight in mills and granaries. Remains of a similar pest, the flour beetle, have been found in an Egyptian tomb dating back 4,500 years.

Mealworms are also fed to birds, reptiles, and—of course—fish, as anglers will know. They are safe for humans who practice entomophagy (the consumption of insects), and are a good source of protein, fat, and fiber. Mealworms may have a useful future beyond nutrition, as they are capable of eating and digesting polystyrene and other plastic waste.

While comical, at least the warning on the box was sensible, unlike some others. The manual for the TraveLite baby stroller advised "Remove child before folding"; Revlon cautioned their customers, "Never use hair dryer while sleeping"; and Aim 'n Flame included small print on their fireplace lighters saying "Do not use near fire, flame, or sparks."

TOM—4 Clues My first thought was a swarm of bees. Close, but not quite. I'd never have guessed that the "supplies" were insects; even after I knew it was birds, I thought it was human food that attracted seagulls or crows.

Scan to see the warning label.

QUESTION

In the days when moveable type was assembled by hand, typesetters used a case with many small compartments to store the individual metal letters. Why did the section containing the capital letters end "T, V, W, X, Y, Z, J, U"?

CLUES

- The Roman civilization is partly to blame for this.
- The movie *Indiana Jones and the Last Crusade* is a useful reference point.
- Working at speed, typesetters used muscle memory.
- What order of events would cause this to happen?
- It was inconvenient to change a previous layout.

SOLUTION

J and U were late additions to the alphabet.

Question submitted by Brian

NOTES

Working by hand over many years, typesetters had developed a knack for instinctively reaching for the correct compartments to grab the right letters. Inserting the J and U in the correct places would have required them to relearn their technique. Instead, they lazily tacked on the additional letters at the end when their use became more common in the mid-1600s.

* * *

The letter J was a very late addition to the alphabet. It was not used in ancient Rome, as either a sound or a spelled letter; the letter I was used instead. Likewise, V was used in place of U. Hence, you will find inscriptions to "IVLIVS CAESAR" instead of "Julius Caesar."

The Italian grammarian Gian Giorgio Trissino is usually credited with suggesting that J should be a distinct letter. He put forward the notion in 1524, though the idea didn't gain widespread acceptance until decades later. Even by 1623, when the First Folio of Shakespeare's plays was published, one title was "THE TRAGEDIE OF ROMEO AND IVLIET." In English texts, J is the third-least used letter, after Z and Q.

In *Indiana Jones and the Last Crusade* (1989), Harrison Ford's character nearly falls to his death when starting to spell JEHOVAH on the stones of a bridge, rather than the intended spelling of the solution, IEHOVAH.

A remarkable number of cartoon characters have the middle initial J, including father and son Homer J. and Bart J. Simpson, Rocky J. Bullwinkle (and his pal Rocket J. Squirrel), Elmer J. Fudd, Philip J. Fry and Hubert J. Farnsworth in *Futurama*, and Stimpson J. Cat from *Ren and Stimpy*.

TOM—5 Clues I figured out the I-J and U-V similarity right away, but I didn't figure out the historical reason until the final clue. I thought it was to avoid accidentally mixing up similar letters.

QUESTION

BEST OF

The Dutch company VanMoof packaged its electric bikes in big, flat cardboard boxes for self-assembly. However, when shipped to the US, many arrived damaged. A trivial change to the packaging caused a 70 to 80 percent drop in damages. What was it?

CLUES

- The packaging didn't require any new padding.
- In fact, the packaging hardly changed at all.
- The trick relied on the rough dimensions of the box.
- The illustration on the box had a little white lie to fool delivery people.
- The new illustration showed something that wasn't inside the box.

SOLUTION

They printed a picture of a flat-screen TV on the box.

Question submitted by Raz Binyamin

NOTES

The company added an illustration of a large television on the box, with the silhouette of a bike added to reassure the eventual recipient. Thinking that the box contained an expensive flat-screen TV, couriers and parcel handlers along the delivery chain were much more careful with the boxes. Overnight, the shipping damages dropped by 70 to 80 percent. Other bike companies later copied the idea.

The idea came from VanMoof cofounder Ties Carlier. The company sold 80 percent of their e-bikes online. After this question was originally featured on *Lateral*, VanMoof was bought out of bankruptcy in 2023 by electric scooter company Lavoie.

■ ■ ■

Bicycles with an electronic component have a long history. Ogden Bolton Jr. patented a battery-powered bicycle in 1895, and two years later Hosea W. Libbey patented a different design that had two different batteries. Both designs were somewhat fatally flawed due to the sheer size of battery required, and the e-bike became viable only when better technologies arrived, such as the lithium-ion battery.

In 2023, more e-bikes were sold in Germany than regular bicycles, and they also outsold EV cars at a ratio of 4 to 1.

Since bicycles are not fitted with speedometers, cyclists can't be charged with speeding in the UK. There is, however, a charge of "wanton or furious cycling"—a criminal offense under Section 35 of the Offences Against the Person Act 1861 (amended 1948).

Scan to see a picture of the packaging.

QUESTION

Noel was gifted a secondhand vehicle by his wife, making it much easier to get around the busy streets of Bristol, England. However, he encountered unforeseen interruptions. How did he circumvent these thanks to a mannequin?

CLUES

- There were no mechanical issues with the vehicle in question.
- What might make Noel's journeys much easier?
- The mannequin was dressed up to look like a person.
- The vehicle was designed for use by a particular profession.
- This vehicle is a common sight around London.

SOLUTION

He made it look like his "taxi" already had a passenger.

Question submitted by Sam Howlett

NOTES

The British television host Noel Edmonds admitted that he used a "black cab" to get around the city. He was able to use the city's special lanes that were reserved for buses and taxis, saving him a lot of time.

Although decommissioned, the taxi still had the classic color and shape of a traditional London cab. This meant that members of the public would sometimes jump into the otherwise empty vehicle and ask to be taken somewhere.

Noel's wife had the idea to dress up a mannequin (which they named Candice) as a real person to ward off pedestrians mistaking him for a genuine taxi driver. When the ruse was discovered by authorities, he swapped to a double-decker bus instead.

■ ■ ■

London's first electrically powered taxis ran in 1897. Called Hummingbirds because of the quiet noise they made, the yellow-and-black cabs had a range of 50 miles—surprisingly sufficient for a day's work. However, the company that manufactured them went bust just three years later.

It's a myth that taxis had to carry a bale of straw with them, though. In the days of horse-drawn cabs, the London Hackney Carriage Act 1831 required drivers to provide food for their steed. The requirement is no longer on the statute books.

Despite the invention of Google Maps, London's taxi drivers still must learn 320 routes within a six-mile radius of Charing Cross, the nominal center point of the city, a skill known as the "Knowledge of London." Passing the Knowledge of London test takes around three to four years.

TOM—5 Clues A roller-coaster ride of a question for me. I thought it could be something to do with Bristol's hills, and then I considered tandem bikes. On the last clue, I finally figured out "black cab." Then I was hit with the surprise that Noel is a famous person.

Scan to read a news article featuring a photo of "Candice."

QUESTION

BEST OF

In 1998, many people bought tickets to the Brad Pitt film *Meet Joe Black*. Handfuls of those people walked out of movie theaters across the US before the film even began. Why?

CLUES

- The people who left were fans of film, at least partially.
- The leavers didn't care about Brad Pitt or *Meet Joe Black*.
- The release of *Meet Joe Black* in 1998 is relevant.
- A major event in movie history was about to happen, but not just yet.
- What happens before the start of a film?

SOLUTION

They'd come just to watch the trailer for another film (*Star Wars, Episode I: The Phantom Menace*).

NOTES

20th Century Fox (now 20th Century Studios) attached the trailer for *Star Wars, Episode I: The Phantom Menace* to *Meet Joe Black*. You had to buy a ticket to the Brad Pitt film to see the trailer. The Star Wars fans in the audience got up and left once they'd seen it.

It is reported that some movie theaters promised to play the trailer a second time after *Meet Joe Black* (all three hours of it) to stop people from leaving early.

The Phantom Menace was released in 1999. It was the first new *Star Wars* film since *Return of the Jedi* in 1983.

■ ■ ■

As their name implies, movie trailers used to be shown after the main picture. However, no one would stick around after the end of the film to watch some advertisements, so they were repositioned to the front of the program. There are now "teaser trailers" that are trailers for the trailers.

Don LaFontaine, also known as the "Voice of God," provided the voiceover for over 5,000 movie trailers. His throaty, deep delivery graced the trailers for *Terminator 2*, *Shrek*, *The Elephant Man*, and *Batman Returns*, among many others.

Swedish director Anders Weberg released a 439-minute-long trailer for his film *Ambiancé*. The full film had a projected running time of 720 hours (30 days) but was never released.

QUESTION

Xavier is driving his car across a long bridge. Halfway across, he notices someone struggling in the river valley 50 yards beneath him. Fifteen seconds later, Xavier saves their life without risking his own. How?

CLUES

- There wasn't enough time to drive the car off the bridge.
- He doesn't jump into the water.
- What kind of distress might the person in the valley be in?
- He has everything he needs to help the person below.
- What does Xavier have that resembles a common piece of lifesaving equipment?

LEVEL 2: MAIN QUESTIONS

SOLUTION

Xavier throws down the spare tire as a life preserver.

NOTES

The person in the river is struggling to swim and is at risk of drowning. Xavier takes the spare tire from his car and throws it over the side of the bridge. The tire is buoyant enough to work as a temporary flotation device.

■ ■ ■

In Michigan there is an 80-foot tire. It was originally built for the 1964 New York World's Fair as a functioning Ferris wheel, with gondolas circulating around the tire's edge.

Your tires may have soybeans in them. As well as being a renewable material, soybean-based compounds provide better traction in rainy weather and last up to 10 percent longer than regular rubber tires. At full speed, the wet-condition tires used on Formula One cars can disperse up to 17 gallons of water every second.

The famous Michelin Man, called Bibendum, is made from white, natural rubber tires, predating the modern technique of adding carbon black. *The Guinness Book of Records* recognizes LEGO as the world's largest tire manufacturer, as it makes over 300 million legitimate solid rubber (if miniature) tires per year.

Bridgestone manufactures 59-inch tires for earthmover trucks used in the mining industry. They have a tread depth of nearly three inches and weigh 11,840 pounds.

TOM—5 Clues I thought there was some misdirection: maybe the person in trouble wasn't in the water, or perhaps Xavier just called for rescue on his mobile phone. I feel like I should have gotten this one earlier.

QUESTION

A hoodie has three things printed on its label: S, XS, and M. What three related words are printed above each set of letters?

CLUES

- S, XS, and M are clothing sizes.
- The missing words are three proper nouns.
- Why might three different clothing sizes be necessary?
- The three words are geographic terms.
- Think about who would be wearing the hoodie, in each case.

SOLUTION

Europe, USA, and Asia.

NOTES

By European standards, the hoodie was regarded as a Small size. Due to different standards for clothing sizes, the same hoodie was a Medium for Asia and an Extra Small for the US.

• • •

When off-the-shelf clothing became more available in the US after World War I, manufacturers found it difficult to get sizing right. Originally, the size number on clothes for children and young ladies reflected the customer's age (e.g., size 16 for a 16-year-old).

As that system became unworkable for different body types, the USDA worked with the Bureau of Home Economics to measure 14,698 women according to their weight and 58 other body measurements, even down to elbow girth and the height of their ankles. However, the survey was flawed as the volunteers were not a representative sample.

Companies are free to use their own sizing schemes, and have been accused of "vanity sizing" by putting smaller-size numbers on the same dress pattern over the decades to flatter their customers.

British shoe sizes are gloriously complicated. To allow for some movement inside the shoe, 0.6 is added to the length of the foot in inches to get the "last length," named after the shoemaker's tool. To obtain the adult shoe size, this number is multiplied by 3 and then 25 is subtracted. The next size of shoe would be longer by a "barleycorn," the English unit for one-third of an inch. The US system is very similar, except that a different number is subtracted at the end (23 for women, 24 for men).

TOM—0 Clues I got this one quickly, after a brief diversion where I was trying to work out why the Roman numerals for ½, 10½, and 1,000 would be printed there.

QUESTION

During an international soccer match one evening in May 2018, the Tunisian goalkeeper lay down on the ground during the second half so that the rest of his team could run off the pitch to find their dates. Why?

BEST OF

CLUES

- The goalkeeper was feigning injury.
- Their Portuguese opponents didn't need the break.
- His teammates were very grateful for the pause in play.
- The "dates" were not people.
- The various timings mentioned in the question are relevant.

SOLUTION

The pause in play allowed the team to break their fast during Ramadan.

Question submitted by Deniz Montagner

NOTES

This friendly match between Portugal and Tunisia took place on May 28, 2018. As it was during the month of Ramadan, Muslims are required to follow "sawm"—a Pillar of Islam where no food or liquid is permitted between sunrise and sunset.

When the sun had set, the goalkeeper pretended to be injured. While he was being "treated," the Tunisian players ran off to their team bench to drink water and eat dates, a common way of breaking their fast. Other traditional "iftar" meals include biryani, samosas, and mango lassi.

The stoppage had the desired effect. Six minutes after the "injury break," Tunisia scored to bring the final result to a 2–2 tie. Tunisia did the same thing a few days later, in another friendly match against Turkey.

■ ■ ■

Ramadan is the ninth month of the Islamic calendar, which is based on the lunar year of 354 days and therefore can happen in any season. Astronomical observers scan the night sky for a crescent moon, using high-powered telescopes from pollution-free vantage points, to pinpoint the moment it starts.

Astronauts on the International Space Station would experience 16 sunrises and sunsets every day. In theory, that would pose a problem for Muslim astronauts, but—as they are counted as "travelers"—they are exempt from fasting.

The end of Ramadan is celebrated with Eid al-Fitr, the Feast of Fast-Breaking.

QUESTION

In 2001, *Nintendo Power* magazine contained a "free demo" of an upcoming Nintendo 64 Mario game. The issue didn't contain any cartridges, electronics, ROMs, download links, or computer code. What was the free demo?

CLUES

- There was no coupon or similar offer for a demo game.
- Some might say it was less a demo and more a simulation.
- What could the "demo" have been made from, physically?
- This prop was extremely low-tech.
- The demo was most definitely "in" the *Nintendo Power* magazine.

SOLUTION

A paper cutout of Mario, to advertise *Paper Mario*.

Question submitted by Sammy Herrera

NOTES

Paper Mario is a role-playing action-adventure game where the player controls Mario as he traverses a land where he and everything around him are made from flat pieces of paper.

When *Nintendo Power* ran an ad for the upcoming game, it included a picture of Mario for the player to cut out and play with, as a very low-tech version of the real game.

■ ■ ■

Mario first appeared as the character Jumpman in the 1981 arcade game *Donkey Kong*, when his creator Shigeru Miyamoto was unable to obtain the rights to license Popeye. Originally, players of *Donkey Kong* were meant to guide Mario around a maze, but there was a superfluous button on the arcade cabinet that allowed for the implementation of Mario's signature jump move. Mario was named after Nintendo of America's landlord, Mario Segale.

In 2021, a buyer paid $2 million for an unopened 1985 *Super Mario Bros.* game cartridge. As the title *Super Mario Bros.* refers to Mario and his younger, taller sibling, Luigi, there has been much debate—both in and outside of Nintendo—about whether this means their surname is Mario, and thus whether Mario's full name is therefore Mario Mario.

Nintendo fans all around the world celebrate Mario Day every March 10 (chosen because "MAR 10" looks like "MARIO"). In 2023, Charles Martinet stood down as the voice of Mario, to be succeeded by Kevin Afghani.

TOM—3 Clues I was hoping it was going to be a full diorama to assemble, complete with pull-tabs to "animate" things!

Scan to see the Mario cutout.

QUESTION

You look at the media cases on a shelf. Three of the titles are *Grand Theft ALEX*, *Call of DRONA*, and *ÄPPLARÖ'S Creed*. Where are you?

BEST OF

CLUES

- The cases are empty.
- One word in each title has been changed to something else.
- What kind of environment would have empty media cases?
- *Super MALM Bros.* is another title.
- You are in a shop known for its sense of humor.

SOLUTION

In IKEA.

NOTES

They are joke titles for fake computer games used as display cases to dress IKEA furniture stores, based on the real video games *Grand Theft Auto*, *Call of Duty*, and *Assassin's Creed*. ALEX is a range of drawer units, DRONA is a storage box, and ÄPPLARÖ is a range of furniture. In the clue, MALM is a chest of drawers.

    Another range of fake IKEA computer game cases uses puns, such as *The Legend of Ingvar*, *Furniture Fantasy VII*, and *Grand Theft Meatballs*.

■ ■ ■

Ingvar Kamprad founded furniture retailer IKEA (which Americans may be surprised to learn is pronounced ee-KAY-uh in Europe) in 1943, naming it after his initials and childhood home (Elmtaryd farm in Agunnaryd village in Sweden). Its $51 billion (€47 billion) revenues from 2023 are larger than the total gross domestic product of Bolivia. Six and a half million BILLY bookcases are sold worldwide every year, which works out to one every five seconds.

    IKEA hackers are people who use the modular parts of IKEA products to make their own designs, a little like LEGO sets. Before online shopping became widespread, the IKEA catalog was one of the most widely read print publications in the world; in 2011, over 200 million copies in 30 languages were distributed across 40 countries.

    When IKEA first opened in the US, customers mistakenly bought flower vases, thinking they were drinking glasses. It's been claimed that one in ten Europeans are conceived on an IKEA bed.

QUESTION

In the 1880s, some hotels had signs reading "This room is equipped with X Y Z. Do not attempt to light with match. Simply turn key on wall by the door." X is a person's name and Y Z is a two-word object. What are X, Y, and Z?

CLUES

- X is possibly the most famous person of the time, and one of the most prolific.
- Y Z is a two-word term for an everyday object or concept.
- People had to be reassured because it was newfangled.
- X is an inventor's surname.
- What is the first thing you often do after opening a hotel room door?

SOLUTION

Edison Electric Light.

NOTES

In the 1880s, Edison's newfangled electric lightbulb was installed in a number of prestigious hotels. No longer did residents have to light a lamp fueled by oil or gas.

The sign was put up to reassure occupants of the room that they could operate the bulb by turning a switch on the wall. It goes on to inform occupants that "the use of electricity for lighting is in no way harmful for health, nor does it affect the soundness of sleep."

■ ■ ■

Thomas Edison didn't exactly invent the lightbulb, but did build on the discoveries of Alessandro Volta and Joseph Swan. He tried bamboo, cellulose, and cotton filaments before settling on carbon. He also realized the importance of a vacuum inside the bulb, and standardized the socket. The most common model of bulb fitting in the US is the E26, where the E stands for "Edison."

Despite his genius, Edison lost the so-called "war of the currents." He preferred direct current, but his rival, George Westinghouse, introduced a network whose alternating current system had several advantages when transmitting power over long distances.

A 4-watt lightbulb at a fire station in Livermore, California, has been lit since 1901, except for two occasions: once in 1976 when it was transferred from the firehouse in which it was originally installed, and once in 2013 when its power supply failed.

TOM—1 Clue I knew the basic concept of this one, thanks to a vague memory of a *Scrooge McDuck* comic book that used this as a gag. I needed one clue to connect it to Edison, though.

Scan to see an image of the hotel sign.

QUESTION

J. M. Barrie's story *Peter Pan* was originally a play and then a book. Over the years, Barrie made various improvements to the story. However, one change—the addition of fairy dust—was required for a non-creative reason. What was it?

BEST OF

CLUES

- It was "required" to prevent a problem.
- In the story, what did the fairy dust allow the characters—including Peter Pan—to do?
- What could be a potential impact of this story on young, impressionable children?
- Thinking backward, what might be the consequences of the fairy dust not being necessary?
- There was a potentially serious safety issue.

SOLUTION

To deter children from injuring themselves, after trying to fly.

NOTES

It was reported that children had started to injure themselves by jumping off their beds and trying to fly unaided. For safety reasons, Barrie changed the story so that the characters could only fly using the special magical fairy dust.

■ ■ ■

Peter Pan was a character that appeared in a series of books and a 1904 play, written by the Scottish author J. M. Barrie. He gave all the rights to Great Ormond Street Hospital. No one knows how much they generate, because the author asked for it never to be revealed.

Although it previously existed, the forename Wendy was popularized through the character in *Peter Pan*. The character was inspired by Margaret Henley, a young girl who called Barrie "Friendly," but this sounded like "Fwendy" as she couldn't pronounce her R's.

In Kensington Gardens, London, there is a statue of Peter Pan blowing a trumpet while standing on top of a tree stump. Barrie lived across the road from the park and featured it in his novel *The Little White Bird*. Unfortunately, Barrie didn't think the statue conveyed Peter's character authentically.

Like James Bond and Bertie Wooster, Peter Pan's nemesis, Captain Hook, was educated at Eton College. In the original play, Hook's final words are "Floreat Etona" ("May Eton Flourish"), the school's motto.

The title of *Quality Street*, a comedic play written by Barrie earlier, was used for a British chocolate assortment brand.

QUESTION

You can buy a plastic novelty that's shaped like an Italian-American mobster. It will play one of four different tunes when floating in water. What is it for, and what is the mobster called?

CLUES

- It gradually plays a symphony of four different tunes.
- Part of the novelty's backstory provides a clue to its use.
- Its first name is shared by a famous mobster.
- It is used in the kitchen.
- The novelty is used in boiling water.

SOLUTION

a. As a timer when cooking pasta.
b. Al Dente.

NOTES

This is a musical pasta timer called Al Dente. The device is added to boiling water together with the pasta. After three minutes, enough to cook angel-hair pasta, the timer will play "That's Amore." It plays the theme from *The Godfather* after seven minutes, enough to cook pappardelle. Further tunes are played at nine minutes and eleven minutes.

Al dente means "to the tooth," where the pasta is cooked just enough so that it retains some bite.

■ ■ ■

It's a myth that pasta was brought back from China by Marco Polo—it was either invented independently or adapted from a version introduced by Arab traders in the 8th century. Most commercial pasta is made from semolina and water, with no egg.

Strozzapreti are short, twisted rods of pasta. The name means "priest chokers" in Italian, perhaps because it was made to spite clergymen who were given the pasta as partial payment for land rents. Fare la scarpetta—"make the little shoe"—is the ritual of mopping up the last bit of the pasta sauce with some bread.

In 1957, the BBC current affairs program *Panorama* broadcast an April Fool's Day hoax showing a Swiss family harvesting strands of spaghetti hanging from trees. Viewers contacted the BBC to find out where they could buy spaghetti trees.

TOM—STUMPED Complete strikeout on this one for me. I figured out "Al" as the first name, but despite that and the "boiling water" clue, I could not make the connection. Hopefully you had more luck than me.

QUESTION

From 1979 to 2007, the residents of the North American town of Naco held a famous volleyball match each April. In the early years, the ball was in danger of bursting. The annual tradition stopped when conditions became too difficult to play. Why?

BEST OF

CLUES

- The game was a way of bringing the community together.
- The geographical position of the town is relevant.
- The ball often used to burst due to what divided the courts.
- It was a home fixture for both teams.
- The "net" was a rigid structure.

SOLUTION

The town played volleyball over the US-Mexico boundary fence, which later became too high to play.

NOTES

Naco lies on the US-Mexico border. When the town was divided into two by the construction of a border fence, locals defiantly started to play volleyball over it, using the fence as their "net." Since the border fence had barbed wire across the top of it, locals had to cover it with carpet to prevent the ball from getting punctured.

The fence was replaced with a much taller version, making the game extremely challenging to play. Although impromptu games still break out occasionally, the last "proper" match was in 2007.

■ ■ ■

Like basketball, volleyball was invented at a YMCA. In 1895, William G. Morgan devised the rules of what he originally called "mintonette"—a call-back to badminton.

Volleyball teams have six players—three at the back of the court who can set the ball for the three near the net, who are allowed to "spike"; that is, hit with a downward motion. Opponents can put up a wall of hands to block shots. A libero is a specialist defensive player who wears a different-colored jersey; they are particularly good at "digging" difficult balls and passing them to the other players.

Even though beach volleyball has two players per side, the court is only 20 percent smaller (and made from sand, of course). In 2021, the Norwegian women's beach volleyball team was fined €1,500 (about $1,600) for wearing shorts instead of bikini bottoms. At the Paris 2024 Olympics, shorts became acceptable for both men's and women's teams.

Wilson is the volleyball that Tom Hanks talks to in the 2000 film *Cast Away*. Wilson has its own profile page on the film website IMDb, and shared a 2001 MTV Movie Award nomination with Hanks for "Best On-Screen Team."

Scan to see more about the Naco volleyball matches.

QUESTION

In Tallinn, these items are found in the same glass display case: knitting needles stuck in a ball of yarn; a rolling pin; a 160-watt-hour battery; and a grapefruit-sized rock. What is it for, and why was a large bottle removed from the case?

- -

CLUES

- This isn't an artwork and the items are not intrinsically valuable.
- The needles, not the yarn, are the relevant bit of the first object.
- Thousands of people walk past this display every day.
- This display helps to explain an important rule.
- Another item in the case is a gun.

SOLUTION

a. To explain prohibited items of hand luggage.
b. The "100 ml of liquids" rule has now been relaxed.

Question submitted by Anna

NOTES

To help passengers understand what items are prohibited in hand luggage, Tallinn Airport in Estonia installed visual representations of things that were not allowed.

The knitting needles are an example of a sharp object, the rolling pin and rock could be used as blunt weapons, and large batteries are a fire risk. Other items in the case are a gun, knives, aerosols, and lighter fluid.

The missing bottle was over 100 milliliters (3 ounces), to demonstrate the rule of carrying any liquid or gel over that size. Some airports, including Tallinn, have recently installed improved security machines that allow this restriction to be removed.

■ ■ ■

The standard type of airport-bag scanners use X-rays, with the resulting images being colorized to distinguish among organic, nonorganic, and metallic objects.

Transportation Security Administration–approved luggage locks became a lot less secure when a close-up picture of the TSA's master keys was printed in a 2014 newspaper article.

TOM—4 Clues I had my suspicions about this one on "160-watt-hour battery," because I knew that was the limit for airport security—but I couldn't connect it to the rolling pin or the missing bottle.

QUESTION

In 1920, some US juice manufacturers would sell their wares as a "brick." People could add the brick to a gallon of water to reconstitute the juice. On the packaging was a warning that virtually all their customers would ignore. Why?

BEST OF

CLUES

- The warning was written with "a nod and a wink."
- The juice could turn into two possible liquids.
- To many, one of these products was more desirable than the other.
- The raw material was grape juice.
- The year is a vital clue. What was going on in 1920?

SOLUTION

The warning was telling customers how to avoid turning their grape juice into wine.

NOTES

During the Prohibition era, vineyards turned their produce into bricks of grape juice, which were entirely legal to sell. One such said "Warning: After dissolving the brick in a gallon of water, do not place the liquid in a jug in the cupboard for twenty days, because then it would turn into wine." Another advised: "To prevent fermentation, add 0.1% Benzoate of Soda."

Of course, most people ignored the printed "advice" and enjoyed the wine.

■ ■ ■

The period of Prohibition in the US didn't ban the drinking of alcohol. Instead, its manufacture, transportation, and sale was restricted with the 18th Amendment to the US Constitution, which ended with the 21st Amendment in 1933. Local laws could still apply—in Mississippi, for example, the possession of alcohol wasn't fully legalized until 2021. Advocates for a dry country believed the barley used in brewing beer could then be used to make bread to nourish people, but in reality, Prohibition significantly increased organized crime.

John Pemberton developed a cure for nerves and headaches that he called Pemberton's French Wine Coca. When Atlanta introduced its own prohibition law in 1886, he removed the wine and just sold the coca drink instead—what we now call Coca-Cola.

British Prime Minister Winston Churchill was a prolific drinker, particularly of Pol Roger champagne. It is thought he drank two pint-sized bottles per day. When he visited the US during Prohibition, he had a doctor's note prescribing alcohol for medical reasons.

QUESTION

Three hundred and fifty-one individuals and organizations were nominated for the 2023 Nobel Prizes, with the winners getting $1 million in addition to the prestige. Why is it rare to hear complaints from nominees, past or present, that they didn't win?

CLUES

- They aren't paid off or threatened.
- It is rare, but not impossible, for people to share their regrets.
- Why wouldn't this be a topic that comes up often in, say, interviews?
- Isn't it surprising that no one complains about missing out on $1 million?
- The Nobel Committee chooses to operate on a certain communication basis.

SOLUTION

The nominees didn't know of the nominations themselves.

NOTES

The Nobel Foundation's statutes insist that any nominations are made in secret. They do not release any information about the nominations, even in private, for 50 years. The winners are chosen by the Nobel Committee, and an announcement is then made. The other shortlisted candidates remain unaware that they were being considered.

■ ■ ■

The prize money comes from a fund established in Alfred Nobel's will—worth around $160 million in today's money. He made his fortune from three inventions, all explosive: dynamite, gelignite, and a "blasting cap" for detonating nitroglycerine.

Six Nobel Prizes are awarded each year—for Physics, Chemistry, Literature, Economic Sciences, Peace, and "Physiology or Medicine." Curiously, there is no prize for Mathematics, which has been the subject of much speculation over the years. Since 1981, the actual medals are made from 175 grams of recycled 18-carat gold, except for Economics winners, who receive a 185-gram medal! (The design is different because it is not one of the original five awards established by Nobel.)

To prevent their confiscation, Hungarian chemist George de Hevesy dissolved the Nobel medals of Max von Laue and James Franck when Germany invaded Denmark in 1940. The gold was precipitated from the aqua regia solution after the War so that the medals could be recoined.

New laureates receive their prize at a special event held on December 10, the anniversary of Alfred Nobel's death.

TOM—0 Clues I knew this one. It's just one of those obscure facts that rattles around in my head.

QUESTION

In 2015, officials from San Francisco's Public Utilities Commission confirmed that dogs had caused a car to be destroyed, nearly killing the car's owner. How?

BEST OF

CLUES

- The car was crushed.
- Name some types of "public utilities."
- The car was damaged by a large object that fell over.
- How could dogs interfere with a piece of street furniture?
- Over time, a large object was weakened without any physical force.

SOLUTION

The dogs corroded a lamppost by urinating on it.

Question submitted by Lateral *guest Nicholas J. Johnson*

NOTES

Dog urine accelerated the corrosion of the metal base of the streetlamp. The pole fell over onto a car, narrowly missing the driver. Several similar events have occurred.

The issue is a major headache for public authorities all around the world. In 2003, Derbyshire County Council in England paid £75,000 (about $95,000) for a monitoring scheme for their one million lampposts. In 2018, it was found that several lampposts in Richmond, Tasmania, had holes in their base, caused by dog urine.

■ ■ ■

Ancient Romans used urine to clean wool and remove the oils from it—a process called "fulling." Believing in this cleansing effect, some Romans used urine as a kind of mouthwash to brighten teeth. Tanners also used it to make leather, and it was also a good fertilizer for farmers. Such was its importance that the emperor Vespasian put a tax on urine to help balance the books.

Astronauts have to recycle their urine. Water recycling rates on the International Space Station are now as high as 98 percent. NASA aerospace engineer Jill Williamson says that it has been "reclaimed, filtered, and cleaned such that it is cleaner than what we drink here on Earth."

It's a myth that you should urinate on a sting after being attacked by a jellyfish. It can provoke the stingers into releasing more venom.

LEVEL 3

The Origins of *Lateral*

As titles go, *Lateral* is a pretty decent one. Most people have a rough idea of what "lateral thinking" involves. The term was originally coined by Edward de Bono to describe how to find creative solutions to unusual problems. The title *Lateral* succinctly gets across the key notion that this show is a bit... different.

Some people assume that lateral and logical thinking are polar opposites, when in fact they are close bedfellows. If a practical problem—like changing a smashed incandescent lightbulb without cutting your hand—needs to be solved, it requires a practical solution. A logical method would be to use some thick gloves. But what if you don't have anything nearby to protect your hands?

Essentially, lateral thinking involves coming up with innovative solutions that are non-obvious, and that may have never been tried before. In this example, you could cut a raw potato in half and place it on the broken lightbulb, then twist it out. This is an entirely logical solution, just not the first one that most people will have thought of.

Lateral started out as a rather different format: a short, six-episode series for Tom's YouTube channel. Each game featured two teams of two contestants, seated behind desks, scoring points against the clock. These shows were released in 2018 and received hundreds of thousands of views.

Despite this initial success, the money from YouTube streams wasn't enough to cover the costs. However, we thought that *Lateral* had legs as an ongoing format, and Tom was looking to start a podcast project as a way of diversifying away from YouTube.

An unforeseen consequence of the COVID-19 lockdown period was that many of our intended guests now had webcams and professional microphones. Recording the show remotely would allow for a wider range of guests than those within traveling distance of London. It also had the bonus of making it relatively easy to capture video for social clips.

A key feature of the British style of panel game format is that points don't really matter, if a score is even kept at all. Also, it was felt that the guests would perform better if they could work collaboratively rather than compete against one another. So, the time limits and points were replaced with an easygoing format where the contributors took turns "hosting" a question. The guests (and Tom) still gained pleasure from key breakthroughs, but the real prize was the friends we made along the way. A pilot was recorded with Rowan Ellis, Pete Donaldson, and Matt Parker, and it was clear that the show had something.

The first *Lateral with Tom Scott* podcast was released on October 14, 2022, with Matt Parker reprising his role as a "first guest." He was joined by the popular Australian pair of Bill Sunderland and Dani Siller, who have been on the show many times since. It still stands up as a very entertaining first show today, which is something of a relief. When running a podcast, new fans are finding the show all the time. One logical—if unexpected—quirk is that, if newly recruited listeners like what they hear, they often go back to Episode 1 and work their way forward. So, we're grateful to Matt, Bill, and Dani for getting us off to a solid start.

In January 2024, the show received its silver "Play Button" Creator award from YouTube. *Lateral* has appeared in the Top 10 of the podcast comedy charts across the world, from Hungary to Argentina, India to New Zealand. Millions more people have sampled the show through social media on TikTok, Instagram, and Facebook. Now, finally, we're proud to bring you the *Lateral* experience in book form.

—D. B.

Warm-Ups

1

Why was the small California town of Yreka once famous for its local bread factory?

CLUES

- What would you normally call a place that makes bread products?
- There's a wordplay trick to this.

2

In the art world, it's claimed that masterpieces long held in private collections can suddenly appear on the open market due to "the three D's": Death, Debt, and ... what?

CLUES

- It's a major life stage, for some people.
- In what circumstance is selling a painting an easy option to solve a problem?

3

Some brands of pear brandy are sold with a whole intact pear inside the bottle. How do the manufacturers achieve this?

CLUES

 It has nothing to do with vacuum pressure.

 The method works, but it takes time.

4

Why did Elvis Presley's manager sell badges that said "I Hate Elvis"?

CLUES

 Obviously, he didn't hate his own star.

 If he didn't provide this service, who would?

5

Why does the University of California, Berkeley, have parking spots marked "N L RESERVED"?

CLUES

 "N L" represents a two-word phrase.

 What kind of person might a university want to honor?

SOLUTIONS

1 Its sign read "YREKA BAKERY"—a palindrome.

The gold-rush town of Yreka was incorporated in 1857. The palindrome is a coincidence, since the town was named after a Shasta Indian word for "north mountain."

An advertisement from 1863 said "Spell 'Yreka Bakery' backward and you will know where to get a good loaf of bread." The bakery closed in 1965 when the head baker retired.

2 Divorce.

Since a painting can't be physically owned by two people, often an art collection is sold off after a divorce so that the proceeds can be split between both parties. Some of these categories have subtleties within them. For example, people might request a valuation so that they can do "estate planning" in the event of their death. Similarly, the collateral of a painting's value can be used to leverage a debt.

3 The bottle is tied onto a tree branch.

The bottle is tied onto a pear tree with a branch inserted into the bottle. The pear grows inside the bottle. The tradition was invented in Alsace, France, in the 1700s.

4 To make money.

Knowing that there would be a sizeable backlash against such a huge phenomenon as Elvis, manager Colonel Tom Parker thought he might as well make money from people who felt that way.

5 They're reserved for Nobel Laureates.

Polish poet Czesław Miłosz asked for, and was given, a parking spot when he won the Nobel Prize in Literature in 1980. The tradition has continued since. There's no such arrangement at UCB's rival, Stanford.

Main Questions

QUESTION

In January 2022, the Miami office of the National Weather Service warned residents (and not for the first time) that they might be surprised by iguanas. Why?

CLUES

- The iguanas are doing something involuntary.
- Iguanas are not native to Florida but have mostly adapted to the environment.
- The iguanas will appear suddenly and without warning.
- How can the weather in January affect an animal's metabolism?
- Where do iguanas often like to spend time?

SOLUTION

The cold weather could make them fall out of trees.

NOTES

Florida is known to have sudden cold snaps around January or February, with temperatures sometimes dipping below freezing.

Unused to such conditions, the non-native green iguanas will experience paralysis. Anyone walking in the area may be startled by the sight of "frozen" iguanas falling from the trees. City streets strewn with iguanas make life difficult for drivers and cyclists.

■ ■ ■

The usual temperature in south Florida is 68°F (20°C), but the metabolism of the iguanas slows down when it falls below 40°F (5°C). They are a significant hazard, weighing up to 20 pounds and measuring up to 3 feet in length.

A sudden drop in sea temperatures also affects the population of Florida's sea turtles. As the waters of coastal bays and lagoons get chillier, they are "cold-stunned" and sometimes found in a comatose state on the shoreline.

Iguanas have a so-called "third eye" on the top of their head. The parietal photosensory organ detects the movement of any predators above them. If something grabs an iguana's tail, it will break at a built-in weak point and eventually regrow, possibly with a different shape or color. Marine iguanas seen around the shores of the Galapagos Islands can hold their breath for up to one hour.

Many types of animals can be picked up by passing tornadoes and deposited hundreds of miles away. In 1921, it rained frogs in Calgary, Canada, and fish fell in the desert of Australia's Northern Territory in 2010.

TOM—4 Clues Initially, I was assuming that the iguanas would be trying to get into people's houses for warmth.

QUESTION

In a thrift store, Simon finds a rubber stamp that is an identical model to one used in offices all across the US. Although there are no identifying marks on it, how does he know it probably came from a school?

CLUES

- Nothing on the stamp bears any text that gives away the institution where it was used.
- The stamp has been used.
- The stamp has moving parts.
- What do you use with a rubber stamp?
- The placement of the ink gave it away.

SOLUTION

It was a date stamp with no ink on JUN and JUL.

NOTES

Date stamps have movable sections for the day, month, and year. The rubber ring that contained the months had no ink on JUN and JUL. This implied that it hadn't been used to stamp any documents during the summer months when US schools are closed.

■ ■ ■

Rudimentary rubber stamps were used by Native Americans to mark their body with patterns that they would later tattoo. Alternatively, printed patterns such as birds, flowers, and tribal symbols could be used as temporary tattoos. In the Philippines and Australia, traditional tribal tattoos sometimes have soot from burnt rubber added to them. In a pinch, this soot might be sourced from used tires.

    The Egyptians used carved "seal stones" as a way of stamping designs of people or written characters into clay. Cylinder seals allowed the pattern to be repeated many times.

    Hard-wearing rubber stamps didn't become possible until Charles Goodyear accidentally discovered the process of vulcanization in 1839 by adding sulfur.

    Railway companies in the UK use special date stamps to reduce fraud. It would be quite easy to change a valuable season ticket to read "JUL" instead of "JUN," so instead, July is stamped as "JLY." Other months are changed (e.g., JNR, FBY, MCH . . .) so that forging a ticket would require a custom rubber stamp. This tradition continues on modern printed tickets.

TOM—2 Clues My first thought was that the stamp was different somehow. As soon as I learned that the stamp was used, everything clicked into place.

QUESTION

In 1935, the US bombed outside the city of Hilo, Hawaii, for one week. Why?

CLUES

- As the bombing was outside the city, no buildings were affected.
- Locals were grateful for their efforts.
- The locals were being saved from a particular threat.
- It was something of a slow-moving threat.
- The geology of Hawaii is highly relevant.

SOLUTION

Geologists arranged for bombs to be dropped on a nearby volcano to slow the flow of lava.

NOTES

Bombing runs on Hawaii's Mauna Loa, the largest volcano on Earth, were ordered to try to save the city of Hilo. The US bombers were commanded by future general George S. Patton (then a lieutenant colonel).

It was later felt that the bombs were not big enough to make much difference, but Mauna Loa stopped erupting in time for it not to matter.

■ ■ ■

The size of volcanic eruptions is graded by the Volcanic Explosivity Index, which runs from 0 to 8. The descriptors for the five most severe levels are cataclysmic, paroxysmal, colossal, mega-colossal, and apocalyptic. The most recent level 6 eruption—Mount Pinatubo, Philippines, in 1991—ejected ten times more material than Mount St. Helens in 1980.

All 30 of the world's highest volcanoes are in South America, as they are higher than Tanzania's Kilimanjaro. The summit of Chimborazo in Ecuador is the farthest point from the center of the Earth, higher than Mount Everest. This is because the world is an oblate spheroid, which means it's flatter at the poles than at the equator. In something of a paradox, there are more than a dozen other volcanoes that are even higher than Chimborazo.

The largest volcano in the solar system is Olympus Mons, a shield volcano on the surface of Mars. As high as two and a half Mount Everests, it has a relatively gentle average slope of 5 percent. However, the hike would be very long, equivalent to walking across the central belt of France.

QUESTION

Near Strasbourg Cathedral, a pink sandstone column stands a short distance away from the corner of a building. Called the Büchmesser, the column was used by city leaders after they renewed their oaths each January. What was its purpose?

CLUES

- The column is situated 14 inches from the building.
- The column was used for a non-architectural purpose.
- The councilors would stay together after renewing their oaths.
- They would celebrate in the evening.
- The column was used as a kind of check.

SOLUTION

To see if they had overindulged in their celebrations by overeating.

Question submitted by Moonlight

NOTES

Each January, the city councilors of Strasbourg would gather for a feast night celebrating Schwörtag, the day they renewed their constitutional oaths.

Built in 1567, the sandstone column was situated near the corner of a building, providing a natural gap which was used as a rudimentary fitness test. If a councilor couldn't fit through the 14-inch gap between the column and the building, they knew they had to go on a diet.

Büchmesser is High German for Bauchmesser; it means "belly measurer."

■ ■ ■

Constructed in the 12th century, a monastery in Alcobaça, Portugal, has a similar design feature. The doorway to the kitchen is only 12.6 inches wide. If a monk was too hefty to retrieve his food from the kitchen, he had to fast until he could get through the gap.

The town of High Wycombe, England, has an annual tradition of weighing the mayor in a public ceremony. Dating back to medieval times, the procedure ensures that the mayor is not overindulging at the public's expense.

A cat's vibrissae (whiskers) are roughly proportional to their body size, so can be used to judge whether they will fit through a narrow gap.

The Lærdal Tunnel in Norway, on the link road between Oslo and Bergen, is another passage that takes effort to get through—because of its length rather than its width. At 15.2 miles long, it's the longest tunnel in the world. It has chambers lit in blue and yellow to help combat the feeling of claustrophobia.

TOM—STUMPED If I knew German, that would have been easy. Even on the last clue, I thought it was a vertical pole to check if they could stand upright after too much drinking.

QUESTION

In 2022, Ipsos polled the British public, asking if they recognized the candidates for leader of the Conservative Party. Six percent of those polled said they were "very familiar" with Stewart Lewis, compared to 5 percent for Suella Braverman, Kemi Badenoch, and Tom Tugendhat. Why was this curious?

CLUES

- Ipsos regularly asks people for their opinions on Stewart Lewis.

- The three people polling at 5 percent weren't scared of competition from Lewis.

- Nevertheless, they would find it embarrassing to be so low.

- It was a sensible measure to include Lewis in the poll.

- Lewis has never been in the Houses of Parliament.

SOLUTION

Stewart Lewis doesn't exist.

NOTES

Ipsos regularly includes Stewart Lewis in their polls as a control measure. It is particularly useful as a baseline in polls asking whether people have a positive or negative perception of a politician.

A similar poll in 2024 found that the number of people recognizing Stewart Lewis had fallen to 5 percent.

■ ■ ■

Early opinion polls were run by newspapers and magazines, often on a local level, without much vetting of the people being asked. In 1936, George Gallup used a more scientific sample to correctly predict that Roosevelt would win his re-election campaign.

A famous photo from November 1948 depicts a beaming Harry Truman, holding aloft a copy of the *Chicago Daily Tribune* bearing the headline "DEWEY DEFEATS TRUMAN." The blunder came about partly because opinion polls were unanimous that Thomas Dewey was going to win the presidential election by a landslide.

Opinion polls work due to a mathematical principle called the Law of Large Numbers. For the US population, polling 1,500 people is sufficient to get the correct result to within 3 percent either way. It is the same phenomenon that tossing a fair coin has a better chance of the expected 50/50 result if you flip it more times.

Ohio is the leading "bellwether" state in US presidential elections. Since 1896, the result of the state's vote has predicted the president every time except for 1944, 1960, and 2020—a hit rate of over 90 percent.

TOM—0 Clues I've run polls before and have included questions exactly like that, just to check whether people were paying attention.

QUESTION

When the game *Among Us* gained popularity in 2020, it was discovered that it had been in violation of the Geneva Conventions for two years. Why?

BEST OF

CLUES

- The same issue has happened to other games in the past.
- It relates to one of the rooms on the spaceship.
- That room is the MedBay.
- Part of the design is protected by law.
- What symbol had they carelessly put in the game?

SOLUTION

The Red Cross symbol was on the wall of the MedBay room.

Question submitted by Francesco Falcone

NOTES

As part of signing up for the Geneva Conventions, national governments undertake their own local legislation to protect the Red Cross symbol from being misused. After being informed of the issue, the developers of *Among Us* changed the color of the cross to blue.

Among Us is a social deduction game that was launched in 2018.

■ ■ ■

The same issue also affected the games *Prison Architect* and *Theme Hospital* (the latter used a green cross, which was changed to an asterisk). The developers of *Stardew Valley* released version 1.3.32 of their game, the patch note for which reads "Fixed a Geneva Convention violation." The red cross on the nurse's hat on the cover of blink-182's album *Enema of the State* was removed for a similar reason.

Other symbols used by the International Red Cross are the Red Crescent (used in countries with Muslim populations) and the diamond-shaped Red Crystal (as a culturally neutral alternative). The Red Lion and Sun was used in Iran until 1980.

The Geneva Conventions are a series of four international treaties that lay out the ground rules for basic humanitarian treatment during times of war. They afford protection to soldiers, sailors, prisoners of war, and civilians in occupied territory. They were the brainchild of Swiss businessman Henry Dunant, who witnessed the dire conditions and lack of assistance that soldiers faced after the Battle of Solferino in 1859.

QUESTION

Some sherry remains in an unusual gift bottle with an asymmetrical design. Without using any measuring equipment, how can you tell whether the bottle is more than, or less than, half full?

CLUES

- There is no need to measure a length or weigh anything.
- The method mainly relies on visual inspection.
- To counteract the bottle's asymmetry, you need to use all of the bottle's interior.
- Some kind of mark needs to be made.
- What could you do with the bottle physically?

SOLUTION

Mark the bottle's liquid level, then turn it upside down.

NOTES

If the bottle was exactly half full, the air would take up the same space as the remaining sherry.

The method is: Mark the current liquid level, or use your thumbnail to indicate where it is. Now turn the bottle upside down. If the liquid is above the mark, more than half of the sherry is left. Conversely, if the liquid level falls short of the mark, most of the sherry has already gone.

This method works because you are trying to fill both ends of the asymmetrical bottle with liquid.

■ ■ ■

Introduced in 1915, the ribbed pattern of a glass Coca-Cola bottle is a reference to the cacao pod, even though it isn't one of the drink's ingredients.

In 2010, 145 bottles of champagne were discovered at an underwater shipwreck in Finland's Åland archipelago. When experts tried the wine, they were amazed how well it had aged. This has started a trend for so-called "submarine wine," where winemakers deliberately submerge wine in underwater cages for decades to improve its flavor.

A Klein bottle is a theoretical mathematical shape that cannot be manufactured in three-dimensional space. Nevertheless, artists and manufacturers of novelties have tried to simulate the effect by having the bottle's neck pass through itself, meaning that there is no difference between the outside and inside surface, akin to a Möbius strip.

TOM—0 Clues This is one of those questions that's easy to grasp intuitively, but really difficult to explain in simple terms. I got it fairly quickly, and then stumbled over my words for quite a while trying to prove that I understood it!

QUESTION

An advertisement consists of a very large word search. All of the letters are blue, except for one answer—the name JAMES—which is orange. What is the ad's message?

BEST OF

CLUES

- There are 19 other answers in the grid.
- Due to the size of the puzzle, it would take a lot of time to find the other answers.
- The other answers are also names, like JAMES.
- Both colors mentioned are relevant.
- The ad raises awareness of something that could save your life.

SOLUTION

You're more visible when wearing a life jacket.

NOTES

The ad reads: "There are 20 names in this word search. But you only saw one. Wear a life jacket." The blue letters represent the sea, and the JAMES in orange represents someone wearing a life jacket.

The ad was devised for the National Sea Rescue Institute of South Africa.

■ ■ ■

Life jackets only became a necessity when more boats were being manufactured from iron. With a wooden boat, there was enough flotsam to use as a buoyancy aid. Early life jackets consisted of cotton jerseys with balsa wood sewn into them. The model worn by survivors of the *Titanic* contained blocks of cork; there were enough life jackets for everyone on board (3,500 vs. 2,240 passengers), but they couldn't help with the problem of hypothermia. In the 1920s, fiber from a tropical plant called "kapok" became the material of choice.

A small canister of compressed air or carbon dioxide self-inflates a life jacket. The model of life jacket used by Allied servicemen in World War II was given the nickname Mae West because the shape reminded them of the Hollywood actress.

It is possible to turn your trousers into a life jacket. Tie the ends of both legs with a knot, then lift the garment above the water to trap air inside. In 2019, a German tourist who fell into heavy seas off New Zealand was rescued when he used this exact method with his jeans.

Scan to see the advertisement.

QUESTION

When Susan went for a hearing test, there was a noticeable dip in the listening response to the frequency of 1,000 hertz. From this, the audiologist was able to correctly deduce Susan's job. What was it?

CLUES

- Why might the ear respond badly to a particular sound?
- Susan had been doing this job for many years.
- What practical use does the 1,000 Hz frequency have?
- This frequency is used by a particular type of person.
- This role typically involves a lot of technology.

SOLUTION

She is a broadcast audio engineer.

NOTES

The 1,000 Hz tone is used by audio engineers as a test or reference tone. It is used to ensure that the equipment is accurate and can be heard clearly by the intended audience.

Because Susan had spent many years in her job, her ears had gradually learned to "tune out" the test signal somewhat, otherwise known as noise-induced hearing loss (NIHL).

■ ■ ■

Presbycusis, the tendency to lose the ability to hear high frequencies as you age, is the principle behind the Mosquito, a device that produces a 17.4 kHz noise. The unpleasant sound is intended to prevent young people from gathering in public places.

Regarding genuine mosquitoes, the females (the ones that bite you) hum at a frequency of around 500 Hz, but this can be modulated in courtship. The caterpillar stage of the North American walnut sphinx moth can create a whistling sound up to 22 kHz. It expels air through its breathing holes if attacked by a predator. Colombian katydids—insects related to grasshoppers—can chirp at 130 kHz.

Human hearing usually peters out at frequencies beyond 20 kHz, which is meager compared to the range that can be detected by dolphins (up to 160 kHz) and bats (up to 250 kHz).

UK and US orchestras tune to the frequency of 440 Hz, also known as Stuttgart pitch, the A above middle C.

TOM—3 Clues My first guess here was "censor," because the bleep that most traditional productions use to cover profanity is also that standard 1000 Hz test tone.

QUESTION

Why did BBC Radio once broadcast an important appeal for members of the public to send in old postcards and photographs of their holidays abroad?

CLUES

- The documents received were forwarded to a department of the British government.

- They were interested in a particular area of the world.

- This happened in an era long before Google Maps.

- The postcards and other documents sent in were going to be scrutinized for information.

- The appeal was made by a Royal Navy Commander in 1942.

SOLUTION

For reconnaissance of Europe's beaches before invading.

NOTES

On BBC Radio, Commander Rodney Slessor of Britain's Royal Navy Volunteer Reserve asked listeners to look through their photo albums and send in any images of the French coast.

Ten million pictures and postcards were received. The best ones were used to help plot out the territory of France's coastline. Together with their own reconnaissance, the War Office used the pictures to decide where best to target their troops on the D-Day beach landings on June 6, 1944. Some postcards were copied in packs given to the soldiers so that they could understand the terrain they would face.

■ ■ ■

It was believed that a postcard service originated in 1870 as a way for Austrian soldiers to send messages back home from the Franco-Prussian War. However, an earlier example was discovered in 2001—a picture postcard sent by the playwright Theodore Hook to himself in 1840, bearing a Penny Black stamp (the world's first adhesive postage stamp).

If deltiology (the collection of postcards) isn't nerdy enough for you, try maximaphily. That's the branch of philately (the collection of postage stamps) where collectors try to obtain postcards that also have a similar person or place on the stamp (and sometimes, the cancellation mark, too).

If you're looking for somewhere unique to post your postcard, you could do worse than the mailbox in Susami, Wakayama Prefecture, Japan. It is 10 meters underwater, a tourist attraction since 1999. Waterproof cards and oil-based pens are used to ensure that your message doesn't wash off.

TOM—3 Clues My first thought was "this had to be a wartime thing," just because the idea of the BBC appealing for old postcards. I needed the third clue to make the D-Day connection, though.

QUESTION

BEST OF

A US company devised its new logo when it had three stores. It planned to update the logo regularly, but soon dropped that idea when the company expanded too quickly. Which company was it, and what was the gimmick?

CLUES

- The planned change each time was relatively minor.
- The idea was abandoned due to the company's rapid expansion.
- The change in question was the addition of a dot.
- The logo now has three dots, all of which feature on one item . . .
- . . . and this item's name is in the name of the company.

SOLUTION

a. Domino's Pizza.

b. One "pip" on the domino for each store opened.

NOTES

Brothers Tom and James Monaghan opened their first "DomiNick's" pizza shop, as it was then called, in 1960. The three dots on the current Domino's logo represent the three original stores that they planned to open in Michigan. However, they soon dropped that plan when they used a franchise model to expand the business quickly.

■ ■ ■

Domino's enjoyed a period of tremendous growth, partly thanks to its famous "30 minutes or it's free!" guarantee introduced in 1984. However, this caused some delivery drivers to be reckless. In 1993, a jury awarded over $78 million in damages to Jean Kinder from St. Louis after she was struck by a Domino's driver, so the company dropped the guarantee.

In the 1980s and 1990s, Domino's had a company mascot called the Noid (short for "annoyed"). Clad in a red costume with rabbit ears, the Noid made cameo appearances in video games and Michael Jackson's 1988 film *Moonwalker*. In 1989, Atlanta resident Kenneth Lamar Noid thought the character was making fun of him personally, and he held two Domino's employees hostage in protest. The incident ended peacefully.

Since 2018, Domino's runs a Paving for Pizza program, where the chain contributes money toward filling in potholes. As well as attracting community goodwill, it makes things safer for its delivery drivers, who clock up to 12 million miles every week in the US alone.

Domino's now has over 17,000 locations in 90 countries.

QUESTION

The German city of Konstanz was one of the few to be untouched by air raids during World War II. While other towns tried to avoid attack by enforcing blackouts, what was this city's clever solution and why did it work?

- -

CLUES

- Konstanz was able to take advantage of its location.
- Its tactic was to confuse the pilots.
- Konstanz is right against Germany's border with another country.
- That other country is Switzerland.
- If this city didn't use blackouts, what logically follows?

SOLUTION

a. To keep the lights on.
b. Enemy pilots thought they were flying over Switzerland.

Question submitted by Jordan Cook-Irwin

NOTES

The townspeople noticed that the nearby Swiss municipality of Kreuzlingen didn't turn off its lights. As Switzerland was famously neutral during the war, it didn't fear attack from either side.

To fool bomber aircraft, they copied the same tactic in the hope that the pilots would naturally assume that Konstanz was also a town on the Swiss side of the border.

■ ■ ■

Although blackouts clearly saved lives, they introduced many other hazards. In Britain, deaths from road accidents rose to 1,130 in September 1939, more than double in the same month the previous year. White arrows appeared on streets in many cities to help people find their way. Pedestrians were encouraged to wear white or carry white things (such as a newspaper) to help visibility.

On trains, passengers were asked to ensure that they were leaving from the correct side of the carriage. The *Daily Sketch* newspaper reported that one passenger was injured from falling down an 80-foot bank, not realizing that his train was merely waiting at a signal before the station. (At the time, train doors opened manually.)

Shops fitted a secondary door—similar to an airlock principle—to prevent light getting out when the main door was opened. ARP (Air Raid Precautions) wardens patrolled the streets of Britain, looking for lit cigarettes and uncovered windows. Blackouts continued until 1944, when they were reduced to a "dim-out."

TOM—5 Clues An infuriating question for me! I've been to Konstanz, I've stood on that border. But I also remembered the town was built alongside a lake, so I was stuck on a water-based diversion until finally the light dawned (pun absolutely intended).

QUESTION

In 1963, Heinz Meixner wanted to drive his girlfriend, Margarete Thurau, back home. In order to do so, he had to take the windshield off his rented sports car. Why?

CLUES

- Heinz was Austrian, while Margarete was German.
- He also let air out of the tires, just to make sure.
- The lovers wanted to elope to Austria, via West Germany.
- Why did the previous clue say "West Germany" and not just "Germany"?
- They had difficulty driving through specific parts of Berlin.

SOLUTION

To drive the car under the security barrier that guarded the entrance to West Berlin.

Question submitted by Ben Tedds

NOTES

Since Heinz was Austrian (a foreigner), he could travel as he pleased. When Margarete (a German native) was refused permission to leave East Germany by the Soviets, the plan was forged. The car Heinz rented, an Austin Healey Sprite, was 35.5 inches high without the windshield. This was two inches lower than the barrier at Checkpoint Charlie.

The escape was a complete success. Heinz drove so fast he left a 96-foot skid mark on the road when he arrived in West Berlin. Margarete's mother was also rescued—she was in the trunk of the car, protected by 30 bricks in case the guards started shooting.

■ ■ ■

The Berlin Wall was erected by the Soviet-controlled East German state to stem the flow of three million migrants who had already crossed into West Germany since 1944. A crude barbed-wire fence was put up overnight by soldiers on August 12, 1961. In its final form, the "Wall" consisted of two concrete barriers, each 100 miles in length.

As the political situation mellowed, on November 9, 1989, politician Günter Schabowski accidentally implied that more relaxed travel arrangements across Berlin were "effective immediately." Huge crowds suddenly gathered at border crossings, and outnumbered guards watched helplessly as thousands crossed.

A 66-yard (60-meter) section has been preserved at the Berlin Wall Memorial. The route of the old wall is marked with a double row of cobblestones. Usain Bolt was given a portrait of himself painted on a 12-foot-high section of the Berlin Wall, weighing three tons, when he broke the 100-meter record in Berlin in 2009.

Scan to read more details about the escape.

QUESTION

In 2015, Saif Siddiqui launched a new type of scarf that became popular with celebrities. His distinctive black and white designs were inspired by an event when a nearby bicycle spoiled something. What is the scarf for?

CLUES

- The exact design pattern isn't relevant.
- One part of the bicycle caused the "spoiling" effect.
- The thing that was spoiled was a photograph.
- The reflective nature of the scarf wasn't a safety measure.
- Other than for fashion, why might celebrities find this useful?

SOLUTION

As an anti-paparazzi measure.

NOTES

In 2009, Siddiqui was posing for a shot, and noticed that the reflector of a nearby bicycle had ruined the photo.

Using the same principle, Siddiqui invented a scarf with a highly reflective pattern. When a photo is taken, the scarf causes the camera's exposure to change so much that anyone in the photo turns into a silhouette. The aim of the brand was to "bring privacy back."

Used by celebrities who want to avoid paparazzi, the scarves cost around $450 each.

■ ■ ■

Tom Baker's iconic multicolored scarf in *Doctor Who* came about by accident. A BBC employee, Begonia Pope, was supplied with a number of different colored yarns. Unsure of the required length, she used up all the wool she had been given to knit a scarf around 20 feet long.

In 2013, David Babcock knitted a 12-foot (3.7-meter) scarf while running the Kansas City marathon in under six hours. He had learned to knit and run after struggling to fit both activities into his lifestyle. Helge Johansen of Norway took 30 years to knit a scarf that was over 15,000 feet (4.5 kilometers), longer than New York's Central Park.

A news photographer is called a "paparazzo" after a character of that name in Federico Fellini's 1960 film *La Dolce Vita*.

TOM—2 Clues I think a cheaper way to do this would be to wear a high-visibility vest, or add some infrared LEDs to your hat, but that's not quite as fashionable!

Scan to see the scarf in action.

QUESTION

A PhD student got two tattoos, one on the middle of each inner forearm. They were circles of different sizes. Why?

BEST OF

CLUES

- The positioning of the circles is important when she stands in a certain way.
- Roughly, the smaller circle is about half an inch in diameter, and the larger one is about two inches in diameter.
- The circles allow her to demonstrate a neat fact.
- She was studying for a PhD in a particular science.
- The two circles both represent something large.

SOLUTION

To demonstrate the relative size and position of the Earth and Moon.

NOTES

Megan Seritan got two circles tattooed on her forearms with diameters that demonstrate the relative size of the Earth and Moon. Furthermore, the locations of the circles were carefully planned. By standing in a "T" pose with arms held out wide, the circles would be the correct relative distance apart.

■ ■ ■

Moon bounce, or Earth-Moon-Earth communication, transmits radio waves by reflecting them off the Moon's surface. Developed in the 1950s, it was successfully used by the US Navy in 1961 when a message was sent from a lab in Maryland to the USS *Oxford* in the Atlantic Ocean, via the Moon. Amateur radio enthusiasts still use the technique.

By firing lasers at reflectors that previous Apollo missions left behind on the Moon's surface, we know that the Moon is drifting away from us at 1.5 inches (3.8 centimeters) per year. It will never "float away," as our Sun will reach its Red Giant phase and engulf both the Earth and Moon before that happens.

The Moon's effect on our tides causes an Earth day to get longer by about one millisecond per century. Billions of years ago, one day on Earth lasted less than 13 hours.

Since this question was featured on *Lateral*, Dr. Megan now has a PhD in planetary science from the University of California, Santa Cruz, and works for the SETI Institute, helping to manage NASA's data from the outer solar system.

Scan to see Dr. Megan's Earth and Moon tattoos.

QUESTION

A British company compiled a list of songs for their customers. The list contained songs such as "Love Me Do" by the Beatles, "Could It Be Magic" by Take That, and "It's Raining Men" by the Weather Girls. Why was this list "efficient"?

CLUES

- The songs share a simple, common attribute.
- The third song contains a slight clue in the title.
- Don McLean's "American Pie" wouldn't be allowed on this list.
- The company wanted their customers to be greener.
- The business was a utility company.

SOLUTION

The song list was designed to help save water by using the songs to time your shower.

NOTES

Thames Water wanted their customers to use less water by taking a shower that lasted only four minutes. They released a list of songs that were all under four minutes long, so that customers could listen to (or sing) them as a gauge of time.

■ ■ ■

"Love Me Do" runs for just 2 minutes and 22 seconds. If you wanted a very speedy shower, you could be clean in just 1 minute and 35 seconds by playing the UK's shortest ever Number One single, "What Do You Want?" by Adam Faith. For those wanting a long soak in the bath, "Blue Room" by The Orb was a UK Top 10 single released in 1992. Its running length of 39:58 was chosen to duck under a 40-minute rule for singles tracks.

A 10-minute shower uses 25 gallons, versus 70–80 gallons to fill a typical bathtub. The first shower was patented in 1767 by William Feetham, a stove maker from London. The catch was that the water had to be pumped by hand into an overhead vessel.

Simple changes can save enormous amounts of water. Fixing a dripping faucet can save 1,450 gallons of water per year. Even just turning off the tap while you brush your teeth will prevent up to 2.5 gallons from going down the drain every minute.

TOM—4 Clues I was confused why Take That's cover was listed, not the longer Barry Manilow original. For a while, I wondered if it was related to the beats per minute, in the same way that CPR compressions should be done to the tune of the Bee Gees' "Stayin' Alive."

QUESTION

On the Netflix television show *Love Is Blind*, contestants go on a series of dates where they cannot see the person they are talking to. Throughout the program, the producers give participants distinctive gold-colored metallic goblets to drink from. Why?

BEST OF

CLUES

- It has nothing to do with product placement.
- What disadvantages would more typical drinking vessels have?
- There is a distinct benefit to the TV production process.
- The various dates can take a while.
- What filming problems do TV and film productions often face?

SOLUTION

To prevent continuity errors.

NOTES

Because the various conversations can take time, producers were worried that the varying liquid levels in the drinking vessels would cause continuity problems when the most interesting parts of the conversation were edited together. By choosing opaque goblets, they removed the problem.

The creator of *Love Is Blind* also told *Variety* that the goblets were a useful way to aesthetically distinguish the series from other shows: "When you turn on the show, you know it's our show."

■ ■ ■

The TV show *Friends* was ripe for continuity problems, as each scene was shot multiple times so that different movements and reactions could be tried out. In fact, some of the takes used in the finished product accidentally feature some of the stand-in actors.

In the film *Pulp Fiction*, bullet holes can be seen in the walls of an apartment . . . before the shootout takes place. In Hitchcock's *North by Northwest*, a child extra in the background covers his ears a few seconds before a gun is fired.

In the film *Pretty Woman*, Julia Roberts is eating a croissant initially, but this becomes a pancake later. *The Simpsons* were caught out when—in a flashback scene—Marge tells Homer that she is pregnant with Maggie. However, there is a picture of Maggie already on the wall behind her.

QUESTION

Karen opens the door to see a delivery driver she's never met before. As she takes her parcel indoors, Karen says to the delivery man, "Sorry about the divorce, but well done on the weight loss." Karen was correct on both counts. What had she noticed?

CLUES

- Both people have never met each other before, and their background doesn't matter.

- There are two parts to this, which rely on two different pieces of evidence.

- What might give away the fact that someone no longer considers themselves to be married?

- Other than baggier clothes, what observation could hint at some lost weight?

- Both answers relate to items worn around the body.

SOLUTION

a. A missing wedding ring.
b. Creases on the belt.

NOTES

The tan line and/or mark left by a recently removed wedding ring would imply that the delivery driver had divorced recently.

A series of creases and/or stretched holes where the buckle would go would be enough to deduce that the driver had recently started wearing the belt tighter after a weight loss.

■ ■ ■

This method of deducing information based on visual clues is known as "hot reading." In a technique requiring less intuition, some mentalists will pickpocket an audience member to, for example, obtain their social security number, and then return the item, so that the number can be revealed as a feat of mind reading later.

The more famous technique of "cold reading" is based on making open-ended statements that can be interpreted in a number of ways. This allows the listener to make assumptions that help mold the statement into something they would agree with, for personal validation.

The Barnum effect, named after the famous showman P. T. Barnum, uses general statements that most people would agree with, such as "Some of your aspirations tend to be pretty unrealistic" or "Security is one of your major goals in life." Often, fortune-tellers begin with such statements and then pick up on a client's verbal and physical cues, while fishing for more information, to mold their reading into something more specific.

TOM—STUMPED I got the wedding ring immediately, but could not figure out the belt.

QUESTION

In 1991, a man lost his house and possessions in a large fire that spread through the Oakland Hills in San Francisco. As a direct result, he developed one of the biggest creative successes in history. What was it?

BEST OF

CLUES

- In a tangential way, fire was part of the creative success.
- What kind of industries is San Francisco known for?
- He created something that involves houses.
- Ironically, his creation sometimes involves fires—but not real ones.
- It's a computer game that's still a massive hit today.

SOLUTION

The computer game *The Sims*.

NOTES

Will Wright, creator of *The Sims*, had already had significant success with titles such as *SimCity*, *SimEarth*, and *SimFarm*. However, when his house burned down, it convinced him of the pleasures of setting up a new home. He added extra fires into the game that were hard to put out—so that the players would need to rebuild their houses just like he did.

■ ■ ■

To greet someone in Simlish, the game's language, say "sul sul." Simlish was originally based on a number of different languages, including Estonian, Ukrainian, and Navajo, but the game's voice actors ended up improvising the majority of the words.

Katy Perry has appeared in *The Sims* as an in-game character, and performed several of her songs in Simlish. The chorus of "Hot N Cold" in Simlish begins something like "Caba hatzi na cou / Fanitsa la bwo / Fanitsi a owl / Fanitsi la dowl." If you throw a successful bash in the *House Party* Expansion Pack, *The Price Is Right* host Drew Carey might arrive in a limousine and join in the fun.

The floating crystal that appears over your character in the game is called a "plumbob." Its color changes depending on the character's mood. Since 2000, *The Sims* franchise has sold over 200 million units. Perhaps it might not have been such a smash hit had they stayed with its working title: *Dollhouse Simulator*.

QUESTION

John drives to the parking lot of his local cinema in Virginia nearly every day. Although this is nowhere near his eventual destination, it saves time for both him and a stranger. How?

CLUES

- The cinema parking lot is one of several places he could have parked.
- If he's not going anywhere nearby, where might he be going?
- The stranger wants to travel the same kind of route as John.
- No money changes hands, yet there is a mutual benefit.
- They are using a feature of Virginia's road network that requires riding together.

SOLUTION

So that they can drive together in high-occupancy vehicle (HOV) lanes.

Question submitted by Hypersmurf

NOTES

John leaves his car at the cinema parking lot and finds a lift to his work.

Like many other US states and countries, HOV lanes encourage people to rideshare. Strangers get to know local landmarks (such as the cinema) where they can pick up passengers wanting to share a ride. This provides a mutual benefit since, traveling together, they can use the less-congested HOV lanes—something they can't do alone.

■ ■ ■

This practice of instant carpooling is known as "slugging" (named after a "slug," bus drivers' slang term for a fake coin). It began in Virginia in the mid-1970s when the Shirley Highway express lanes were implemented, which required four occupants per car at the time. High gas prices in the 1970s also provided an economic incentive to share rides.

In 1987, around 2,500 commuters used this system. A 2019 report claimed that 20 percent of all carpooling in the Washington, DC, area was slugging, though this understandably dropped to 4 percent during the COVID-19 pandemic. A website called *Slug Lines* (now mothballed) contained information about popular slugging routes. It remains a popular scheme with employees from the Pentagon as thousands of people want to travel along similar routes, though naturally that imposes an implicit restriction on small talk.

TOM—3 Clues I got hung up on the "cinema" part of this question for far too long.

QUESTION

BEST OF

Putney Bridge in London is unusual in that it has a church at both ends—All Saints on the north bank of the Thames, and St. Mary's on the south bank. How did that come about?

CLUES

- It has nothing to do with the denominations of the religions of the churches.
- This is a relatively old part of London.
- A river is a natural barrier.
- What is the usual solution for traveling across a river?
- Think about the timeline of events.

SOLUTION

The churches were built before the bridge.

NOTES

There was a Christian worship site on the south bank since the 13th century, and on the north bank since the 12th century. Two churches were built because there was no easy way to cross the river.

The first bridge to connect the two banks wasn't attempted until 1729, making it the second-longest bridge across the Thames (after London Bridge). The current stone bridge dates to 1886.

■ ■ ■

The feminist Mary Wollstonecraft (mother of *Frankenstein* author Mary Shelley) threw herself off Putney Bridge in 1795 when she found out her husband was having an affair with an actress. She was saved by boatmen passing by.

Until the first bridge was built, a ferry service was used. It is said that Prime Minister Robert Walpole agreed to speed up progress for a bridge, after he was making his way back to Parliament and the ferryman was drinking in a pub on the other side of the river.

In 1798, Prime Minister William Pitt the Younger held a duel with William Tierney MP over a parliamentary bill at nearby Putney Heath. Both missed and lived to see another day.

Until 1882, the bridge charged a toll. However, in 1739, 1789, and 1814, the locals were able to cross without paying the toll. The Thames had frozen over, so people just walked across. For most of its long history, Putney Bridge has been the starting point for the annual University Boat Race between Oxford and Cambridge.

QUESTION

The social media site Meetup connects people with similar hobbies and interests. Why is there a disproportionate number of users registered to a General Electric plant in Schenectady, New York?

CLUES

- The issue stems from an assignment made in 1971.
- This situation had to happen somewhere near the East Coast of the United States.
- The app's users were lying.
- The GE plant also receives a lot of mail for the same reason.
- How might people try to hide their real address?

SOLUTION

It has the ZIP code of 12345.

Question submitted by both Robert D. and Bryan

NOTES

Not wishing to enter their real details, many app users lazily enter "12345" as their ZIP code.

The General Electric plant has its own mailroom that sorts the real mail from the fakes. They receive posts addressed to such names as Mickey Mouse, Humpty Dumpty, and Jane Doe. Workers also answer hundreds of "Letters to Santa" that arrive there.

It's estimated that over a million people have claimed to live in Schenectady, compared to the real population of 66,000.

ZIP stands for Zone Improvement Plan. Broadly, ZIP codes start from 0 to 9 as you work from East to West. The codes were introduced by the US Postal Service in 1963, with this GE plant receiving its own code in 1971. At that time, the plant received 50,000 pieces of external mail every day.

■ ■ ■

Another popular choice for those wanting to keep their details private is 90210, after the American teen drama television series based in Beverly Hills.

Eleven percent of bank cards have a PIN of 1234. Researchers analyzed 3.4 million bank card PINs that had been leaked online. The next most popular were 1111, 0000, 1212, and 7777. Month-Day or Day-Month sequences were common (e.g., 0910 or 1009 for September 10), as were years beginning 19 or 20. The sixth-most popular PIN was 1004 because it sounds like "cheonsa" ("angel" in Korean).

TOM—3 Clues I should have got this much sooner as it's right in my wheelhouse: communication infrastructure, power plants, and IT! As it was, I needed three clues.

QUESTION

In 1985, it was reported that some flocks of sheep in the town of Blaenau Ffestiniog, Wales, had been quarantined. Without this safety measure, millions of pounds of infrastructure would have become obsolete. What had the sheep done, and how had they done it?

BEST OF

CLUES

- What sort of infrastructure might the sheep come across?
- They didn't require any extra equipment.
- No teamwork was required.
- Their clever method prevented their hooves from getting caught.
- They used a certain amount of gymnastic ability.

SOLUTION

a. They'd worked out how to cross cattle grids (also known as cattle guards or cattle grates).

b. By tucking in their legs and rolling across.

NOTES

The sheep that learned this stunt had to be kept in quarantine to prevent them from "telling" other animals the same trick. Otherwise, all the cattle grids in the country would soon become useless.

Twelve years later, a group of sheep in Hampshire realized that they could use a self-sacrifice technique—one sheep would lie down on the grid while others scrambled across her.

In 2004, the BBC reported on a flock of sheep in Yorkshire, England, that had also managed to lie on their side and roll across the grid. The flock had also learned to jump over 5-foot fences, and squeeze through gaps as small as 9 inches. A Leicester sheep called Lucy stunned farmers when she was able to put her head through a fence and use her mouth to wriggle a bolt latch open from the wrong side.

■ ■ ■

In 2014, a six-year-old Merino sheep called Shaun escaped from a farm and ended a life on the run when he was eventually found wandering on scrubland. Having never been sheared in his life, his fleece had grown to 23.5 kilograms (about 52 pounds)—which at least made him easy to catch when found.

Studies reported in 2001 showed that sheep were able to remember the faces of up to 50 of their flock as well as the human faces of their handlers.

Another animal that managed to spread a clever "knack" is the blue tit. In 1921, blue tits began to peck at the foil covering on milk bottles in Limerick, Ireland. By the 1940s, their trick was widespread.

What Makes a Good Question?

We work hard to make the questions on *Lateral* as good as they can possibly be. This means that questions have to jump through a number of hoops. First and foremost, they need to be original or at least based on a fact that isn't too commonplace. The most stressful part of my job is trying to predict the questions Tom probably won't get right away!

The next most important question criterion is having a strong "penny drop" moment, where confusion suddenly becomes delight. A good sign is when hearing the solution elicits one of two reactions—a punctuated "Ha!" for inventive or funny situations, or an elongated "Woooow!" if something strange or foolish has happened. As such, *Lateral* celebrates the full range of human "achievement"—from the amazingly brilliant to the unbelievably stupid.

Really great questions have what I like to call the "domino effect." Asking a *Lateral* question is like pushing over the first of a trail of dominoes, and one hopes that the dominoes fall over in the correct order so that the correct solution is reached. The introduction question that you hear in the "cold open" of each *Lateral* episode tends to have just one step or "domino." The main questions tend to have two or three steps or leaps of logic—you hear the question, work one thing out, realize another thing or two, and then you get the answer. Anything more complex feels a little tenuous or, at best, overruns the 10 minutes of studio time available to get through a question.

You may have noticed that most *Lateral* questions are based on real events. Real life is a better source of inspiration of ideas than anything a writer could devise, and a real-world basis helps restrain the possibilities to things that are realistically plausible.

This is why we avoid those "murder mystery" stories that often appear in lateral-thinking puzzle books. Fun though they are, the solutions often seem a bit too bizarre for people to be able to reason out within a tight time frame. Another unsatisfactory downside is that it's often possible to come up with alternative, somewhat plausible, solutions.

Finally, it's always better if there are clues in the question that give the guests some specifics. Names, locations, and years usually offer a useful context. Also, it's unfair if the solution relies on an obscure piece of trivia that isn't hinted at or deducible from some open questioning. The guessers should always say "Ah, of course!" not "Oh, really?" when they hear the solution.

From early on, we've always wanted to include questions submitted by listeners. It's a great way of hearing about neat stories with clever twists, particularly from other countries and cultures. We were initially hoping that perhaps 1 to 2 percent of submissions might be usable, but the real figure is many times this—a testament to the listeners understanding our style very quickly. Every single question submitted is read and logged on a huge spreadsheet. As of this writing, over 5,000 ideas have been submitted so far.

If you have the inkling for a good *Lateral* question, please feel free to submit it to us—we'd love to hear from you. Visit lateralcast.com and click on the "Send in your own question idea" button. That will take you to a form that has detailed instructions on what to do. Who knows, one day Tom might be mentioning your name on the show!

—D. B.

Warm-Ups

1

When offered for sale, what items are described as bumped, foxed, sunned, cracked, and shaken?

CLUES

- These adjectives are describing conditions that can affect the sale price vastly.
- What might have been left in the sun, bumped at the corner, and cracked in one place?

2

Why do the Toronto Blue Jays need two more minutes to get their baseball games underway than if two other MLB teams were playing?

CLUES

- Toronto is the only Major League Baseball team that needs to do this.
- What happens before the start of a sports event?

3

What connects Microsoft Windows, the iPhone, and "7" in a joke?

CLUES

 It has to do with numbers.

 The joke is "Why was 6 afraid of 7?"

4

What sort of person would be interested in buying exactly 1.91 US dollars or 3.88 UK pounds?

CLUES

 The purchase wouldn't be used in a practical sense.

 In all, this would involve the purchase of six different American (or eight British) items.

5

Why did the writer George Bernard Shaw call his garden shed "London"?

CLUES

 He was living 30 miles north of London at the time.

 It was done so that his staff could say a half-truth.

SOLUTIONS

1 Secondhand books.

Bumped: crushed corners. Foxed: brown spots. Sunned: faded from sunlight. Cracked: hinge has a crack. Shaken: pages coming loose from the binding.

2 To play both the Canadian and US national anthems.

The Blue Jays are the only Canadian team in the MLB. When a US team plays at the Blue Jays' stadium, the US anthem is played first, followed by "O Canada." US teams return the gesture when the Blue Jays go on the road. Once, the Chicago White Sox used to start at 7:11 p.m. because of a 7-Eleven promotion.

Question submitted by Anonymous

3 They made "9" disappear.

Microsoft went straight from Windows 8 to Windows 10. The next model after the iPhone 8 was the iPhone 10. A classic joke asks, "Why was 6 afraid of 7?" (Answer: "Because 7 'ate' 9.")

Question submitted by John from Melbourne

4 A coin collector (numismatist).

These amounts are what's required to buy a complete set of the common coins in circulation. The main US coins are the 1¢, 5¢, 10¢, 25¢, 50¢, and $1, which total $1.91. In the UK, the coins are 1p, 2p, 5p, 10p, 20p, 50p, £1, and £2, which total £3.88.

5 When unwanted visitors called at the house, his staff could say, "Sorry, Mr. Shaw is in London today."

The shed was in the garden of his home in Ayot St. Lawrence, Hertfordshire. The shed could turn on casters around a circular track, like a restaurant's lazy Susan, so that it could follow the sun during the day. It also had a fan heater, a telephone connection, and an alarm clock to tell him when it was time for lunch.

Main Questions

QUESTION

At the start of a film shoot in a house, one member of the crew will put their keys in the fridge. Who does this, and why?

CLUES

- The keys don't need to be kept cold.
- It's a common crew member found on almost all film shoots.
- The keys are retrieved at the end of the day.
- The fridge causes a problem for one of the technical film crew.
- The placement of the keys forces them to think about something.

SOLUTION

a. The sound recordist.

b. To remind them to turn the fridge back on.

Question submitted by John Arthur Kelly

NOTES

The hum of a refrigerator, while relatively quiet, is often still picked up by sensitive sound recording equipment on location. As such, it is usually unplugged while a shoot takes place. This is done whenever there is a fridge on location, even if the crew is not filming in the kitchen itself.

The sound recordist will place something they can't leave without, usually their van keys, in the refrigerator as a reminder to plug it back in when the shoot is done for the day. It's a useful hack that's taught at film school.

■ ■ ■

A predecessor of the fridge was the zeer, two nested clay pots with a layer of wet sand between. When the water evaporated, it cooled whatever was in the inner pot.

The first commercial refrigerator that could chill food by a compressor (and not ice) was invented by the Australian James Harrison in 1854. Since it uses tons of liquid helium to cool down its magnets to $-273°C$ ($-456°F$), the Large Hadron Collider is technically the world's biggest fridge (and ironically, also the hottest thing in the observable universe when operational).

In the 2008 film *Indiana Jones and the Kingdom of the Crystal Skull*, Harrison Ford's character survives a nuclear explosion by hiding in the fridge. As a result, "nuking the fridge" has become an updated version of "jumping the shark."

TOM—4 Clues Weirdly, despite being on a lot of video shoots in my time, I've never seen this done—but I'm going to remember it for the future.

QUESTION

In January 1990, two men from Seattle hit on an idea for a new design of eyeglasses. After selling a million pairs, they closed down their company in 2009, after which time their designs would hit a problem. Precisely what did they sell?

BEST OF

CLUES

- Their designs didn't contain lenses, although some of their competitors' did.
- Arguably, their design became more elegant from the year 2000 onward.
- Concentrate on the middle two digits of the year.
- Most of these glasses would only be worn once.
- It's relevant that they hit on this idea in January.

SOLUTION

Novelty "year number" glasses, worn on New Year's Eve.

NOTES

After a music jam in January 1990, two Seattle musicians, Peter Cicero and Richard Sclafani, hit upon an idea for novelty glasses that were made up of a year number. The two "eyes" would poke through the holes in the 9s or—from 2000 onward—from the middle two 0s.

The market became oversaturated with knock-offs, so they left the industry in 2009 after selling a million pairs. However, the numbers from 2010 onward would not have been as easy to design glasses for, since there were no central "holes" for the eyes.

■ ■ ■

The tradition of lowering a ball in Times Square to mark the start of the new year began on December 31, 1907, because a ban on fireworks had been introduced. The tradition of "time balls" was first used by the British Admiralty in Portsmouth in 1829 as a way of marking midday so that ships could adjust their clocks to local time.

New Year's resolutions are said to date back to the Babylonians, 4,000 years ago; they held Akitu, an annual 12-day festival that started on the vernal equinox.

In Spain, people eat 12 grapes—one for each striking of the clock on December 31. Brazilians eat lentils, the pulses representing money. A popular New Year's Eve custom in Denmark is to smash plates and glasses (preferably unwanted ones) against the front doors of friends and neighbors.

QUESTION

Max-Hervé George was one of the most successful share traders in France. His portfolio rose an average of 68 percent per year from 1997 to 2006. When prices were published each Friday, he made a profit from nearly every trade. How?

CLUES

- He is not psychic, nor is there any statistical prediction going on.
- He trades life insurance as a savings product.
- He is taking advantage of technological advancement.
- The insurer made a bad mistake in the past.
- What clause would give you almost perfect hindsight?

SOLUTION

He has the right to buy stocks at last week's prices.

NOTES

In 1987, the company L'Abeille Vie started to offer a deal that allowed people to trade based on the price from the previous Friday. This wasn't a big deal initially, when trades could take days—by which time the market could have changed again. In the internet age, though, deals can be sent instantly. This has the effect that you can trade with perfect information—if the market has risen this week, you can use your right to buy at last week's prices.

    Thousands of these contracts were sold. As a way of getting people to sign away their rights, policyholders were offered 100 francs (worth about $60 at the time) to sign some paperwork, unaware that the paperwork contained new terms and conditions that canceled this right. When George tried to use faxes to speed up his trades, the insurer refused. So, he sent a bailiff each week to hand-deliver his instructions.

    In 2007, Aviva (the company that had bought L'Abeille Vie) began court action to stop this clause. If George prevailed, it was estimated that he could be worth €234 billion by 2030. Aviva later sold its French business in 2021.

■ ■ ■

Aviva can be dated back to 1696, when one of its businesses was the Hand in Hand Fire & Life Insurance Society. Their fire mark—the metal marker that showed which buildings were insured by each company—was a handshake.

TOM—5 Clues I needed all five clues for this one. It seemed so bizarre!

QUESTION

To prevent hitting his head, Tom put a few British £1 coins in his shoes. Why?

CLUES

- "Tom" is not Tom Scott.
- There's nothing specific about the coins themselves.
- However, they were small and dense enough to get the job done.
- Tom wasn't walking on his shoes.
- Many people have seen this balancing act.

SOLUTION

Actor Tom Cruise was using the coins to balance himself in the CIA scene in *Mission: Impossible*.

NOTES

In the famous scene—where Tom Cruise drops from the roof of the CIA's Langley headquarters on a rope and hovers over the floor—Cruise would keep hitting his head. The £1 coins were just enough to adjust the balance so that Tom would come down parallel with the floor.

In *Newsweek* magazine, Tom Cruise explained: "I told them to give me some of those English pound coins and I put them in my shoes. So we did, and I balanced myself that way just off the floor. It felt like an hour, it was probably three seconds. Then Brian [De Palma] said 'Cut' and gave me a hug."

■ ■ ■

Cruise was a fan of the original 1966 *Mission: Impossible* TV series and bought the rights to develop it into a film series. The first film of these was the final major studio release on the Betamax videotape format.

The term "self-destruct" (as in the famous line "This message will self-destruct in five seconds...") was coined by the original TV series. The franchise's trademark scene—where the team builds an entire fake room—is called a "mousetrap" by the producers. Tom Cruise has performed many *M:I* stunts himself, including scaling the Burj Khalifa, clinging to an Airbus A400M, and jumping out of a C-17 military cargo plane...106 times.

In his career, Cruise has clocked $10 billion in worldwide aggregate box office as a leading actor, more than anyone else.

QUESTION

Not a Wake by Michael Keith is a book of assorted literature, including poetry, crossword puzzles, and a movie script. The first line reads, "Now I fall, a tired suburbian in liquid under the trees." What is the book's theme?

CLUES

- The meaning of the first line doesn't matter.
- It's not a coincidence that "Not a wake" and "Now I fall" have a similar appearance.
- "Now I tumble . . ." wouldn't fit the theme, but "Now I trip . . ." would.
- Every single word written posed a limitation on the author.
- Michael Keith is a software engineer and mathematician.

SOLUTION

The lengths of the words represent the digits of pi.

Question submitted by Zorua

NOTES

The mathematical constant begins 3.14159265358979... and continues forever, seemingly without a recognizable pattern. Keith uses the first 10,000 digits to inspire his constrained writing. By counting the letters of each word in the text (discounting punctuation and other symbols), you obtain the digits of pi. Note that the title also represents 3.14.

Not a Wake also includes several short stories and an entire play.

■ ■ ■

Michael Keith also cowrote *The Anagrammed Bible*, which contains anagrams of every verse (or block of verses) from three books of the Old Testament that have the same approximate meaning as the original.

Pi is used for the ratio of a circle's circumference to its diameter because it is the Greek alphabet's equivalent to the letter P, representing "perimeter." Pi Day is celebrated on March 14, due to the 3/14 date. July 22 (22/7, as the date is styled in the UK) is Pi Approximation Day. In 2015, Rajveer Meena recited the first 70,000 digits of pi from memory, while blindfolded.

There is little real-world use for this many digits. NASA scientists say they never need more than 16 decimal places. In the 19th century, Englishman William Shanks calculated the first 707 places of pi by hand in his spare time; in 1944, it was discovered that Shanks had made a mistake at the 528th digit. Google calculated pi up to 31.4 trillion decimal places on Pi Day in 2019.

A lipogram, where the author self-imposes a ban on one or more letters, is another example of constrained writing. A famous example is Georges Perec's *La Disparition* (*A Void* in English), a 300-page novel that does not contain an "E."

TOM—0 Clues I was the sort of nerdy kid who memorized 30 digits of pi with a mnemonic, just because I could. I spotted this by the end of the question.

QUESTION

BEST OF

In Dutch, Afrikaans, and Māori, tea is known as "thee" or "tee." In the Middle East, China, and Russia, it is called "shay," "chai," and "chay," respectively. What caused this popular beverage to have two names worldwide?

CLUES

- You don't need to be a linguist to solve this.
- There is a visual way of linking these countries.
- Imagine the countries mentioned on a map.
- Which country was the first major producer of tea?
- Physically, what happens to a commodity like tea?

SOLUTION

Whether it had been sent by land or sea.

NOTES

Tea that traveled from China by land was named after the Mandarin or Cantonese word "cha." Tea sent by sea was called "tea" or similar, because locals spoke a different dialect of Chinese on the south coast. This is encapsulated in the saying "Tea if by sea, cha if by land."

■ ■ ■

In the mountainous Chinese province of Yunnan, there is the Jinxiu Tea Tree, which is reputed to be 3,200 years old. Legend has it that, in 2737 BCE, some leaves from the *Camellia sinensis* plant fell into a hot cup of water that Emperor Shen Nong was drinking.

Assam, Darjeeling, and Ceylon are black teas, which have been fully oxidized. Green tea, such as matcha, retains its natural color as it has had minimal processing. Oolong tea (meaning "black dragon") is somewhere in between, the leaves being partially fermented before they are dried.

Tea importer Thomas Sullivan provided samples of tea to potential customers by putting small batches of leaves in small silk bags. However, rather than taking out the leaves, the customers put the entire thing in boiling water, and the concept of the tea bag was born.

Iced tea was popularized by Richard Blechynden, who had a tea pavilion at the 1904 World's Fair in St. Louis. During a heatwave, he put ice chips in his black tea drinks to provide a refreshing alternative. Eighty-five percent of tea consumed in the US is served cold.

QUESTION

Why did taxis in Madrid once have to display a window sticker with the letter L, M, X, J, or V?

CLUES

- It's significant that there are five letters.
- The letters are already in the correct order.
- The letters represent the start of something.
- This regulation was to reduce congestion.
- What is a simple way to limit the congestion caused by a fraction of the vehicles?

SOLUTION

They couldn't drive on that day of the week.

NOTES

To reduce congestion and pollution, some cities operate a system where a certain proportion of vehicles are not allowed to drive into the city center.

In Madrid's case, each taxi driver was given a sticker that indicated which day they were banned from entering the city:

- L—lunes (Monday)
- M—martes (Tuesday)
- X—miércoles (Wednesday)
- J—jueves (Thursday)
- V—viernes (Friday)

"X" was used for Wednesday (miércoles) to differentiate it from Tuesday (martes). The history behind this is unclear—it may have to do with Mercury → Merc → Merx → Mx → X.

The regulations were reformed in 2023 so that taxi drivers could operate whenever they wanted, so the letters were no longer necessary.

■ ■ ■

Several other cities have a similar scheme. Since 1989, Mexico City has operated the splendidly named "Hoy No Circula" ("Today does not circulate") system, which uses the last digit of the license plate. To combat periods of high particle pollution, Paris implements its "Circulation Alternée" system, where cars whose plates end in an even-numbered digit can only enter the city on even-numbered days (and likewise for odd).

TOM—4 Clues The X, and five rather than seven letters, completely threw me off the scent here.

QUESTION

Why does a list of #1 albums for the official UK music charts have no entry for the year 1959?

CLUES

- There are several albums listed for the years 1958 and 1960.
- Albums were bought and sold normally throughout the 1950s.
- Likewise, the album chart was compiled normally during 1959.
- What prompts a new entry on the list of #1 albums?
- What would happen if an album was immensely popular?

SOLUTION

Because an album from 1958 remained at #1 for the whole of 1959.

NOTES

No new album became #1 in 1959, so the list goes straight from the last album in 1958 to the first new #1 in 1960.

The original soundtrack for the musical *South Pacific* became #1 in the UK charts on November 2, 1958, and remained there for the next 70 weeks until it was knocked off its perch on March 6, 1960.

■ ■ ■

The *South Pacific* soundtrack was based on the 1949 Rodgers and Hammerstein musical of the same name. An instant critical and commercial hit, it features songs such as "There Is Nothin' Like a Dame," "Bali Ha'i," "I'm Gonna Wash That Man Right Outa My Hair," and "Happy Talk." In total, the soundtrack album spent nearly four years in the Top 5 of the UK's album chart. It was overtaken by "The Explosive Freddy Cannon" by Freddy Cannon; although that record was #1 for just one week, it was the UK's first rock 'n' roll album.

Composer Richard Rodgers, lyricist Oscar Hammerstein II, and book coauthor Joshua Logan won the 1950 Pulitzer Prize in Drama for *South Pacific*. This means Rodgers was the first person to have won the "PEGOT" by earning a Pulitzer Prize, Emmy, Grammy, Oscar, and Tony Award (composer Marvin Hamlisch being the other, to date). The partnership of Rodgers and Hammerstein also won 42 Tony Awards and 13 Academy Awards.

QUESTION

A manufacturer tests its products to a "plus or minus 2" tolerance in five different positions: dial up, dial down, 3 o'clock, 6 o'clock, and 9 o'clock. What does the tolerance mean, and why is 12 o'clock missing?

CLUES

- What common object has a dial?
- What is a frequent problem with lower-tech versions of that object?
- What measurement unit could the "plus or minus 2" refer to?
- What do the 3, 6, and 9 o'clock positions mean?
- Why is it hard to use the item in the 12 o'clock position for long?

SOLUTION

a. A (Rolex) watch doesn't drift more than two seconds a day.
b. It's hard to hold a watch in the 12 o'clock position.

Question submitted by Mitchell Swan

NOTES

The manufacturer is Rolex, which submits their watches for testing by the Swiss Chronometer Testing Institute.

The watches are tested in five different positions:

- 3 o'clock/6 o'clock/9 o'clock—when your arm is by your side, either pointing down, horizontal, or vertically up
- Dial up—as if looking at the watch
- Dial down—with the watch in storage, or on a table facedown

The 12 o'clock position would be as if the watch were vertical, like a clock on a wall. However, it is unnatural for someone to hold their arm in that position for any great length of time.

Rolex says that their watches should not lose or gain more than two seconds a day, in any position. Other manufacturers submit their watches for these tests but may use different tolerances.

■ ■ ■

The Rolex brand was created in 1908 by Hans Wilsdorf and Alfred Davis, the name possibly chosen because it was short enough to fit on a dial and easy to pronounce in several different languages. They looked to champion "wristlets"—wristwatches—at a time when men were using pocket watches. In 1930, their famous Oyster Perpetual was the first self-winding wristwatch on the market.

Rolex's sponsorship of sportspeople has a long history. Mercedes Gleitze was the first woman to swim across the English Channel in 1927, and did so while wearing a Rolex around her neck.

TOM—3 Clues As someone who's now used to sub-second accuracy from phones, laptops, and smartwatches, two seconds per day sounds terrible. That's a whole minute every month!

QUESTION

On certain days, kids in Hong Kong are given a breakfast such as two eggs with a sausage, or an ear of corn with a couple of dumplings. Why?

BEST OF

CLUES

- There are always three main elements to these breakfasts.
- The presentation of the food is key.
- These items could be rearranged into a face. What else?
- On what kind of special days might children need a motivational breakfast?
- You are meant to "read" the food as characters.

SOLUTION

To motivate them to score 100 percent when they're about to take an exam.

Question submitted by Norman Liang

NOTES

The breakfast items are arranged to look like the number 100. There are other presentations, too, such as a hot dog with two piles of rice, or a banana with two donuts.

...

Breakfast hasn't always been a concept. The Romans believed it was healthier to have one large main meal around midday, and frowned upon eating beforehand. In England, breakfast didn't become commonplace for all social classes until the 17th century. An early meal was welcomed by the workers doing hard labor and long hours in the Industrial Revolution. The word "jentacular" is the adjectival form of "breakfast," as in "I took a post-jentacular run this morning."

The traditional "full English" breakfast may have developed from Collop Monday, the day before Shrove Tuesday, when people started to use up their meat before the beginning of Lent. The version sold at Shepherds Place Farm, Doncaster, England, consists of 15 portions each of 10 items: sausages, bacon, hash browns, eggs, black pudding slices, toast, fried bread, mushrooms, baked beans, and tomatoes. The 17,000-calorie feast weighs over 15 pounds and costs £50 ($65).

Despite its status as a French icon, the croissant is likely a version of the kipferl, a crescent-shaped Austrian bread roll. Cornflakes were invented by accident when John Harvey Kellogg left some boiled maize out and it went stale; he pressed some through a roller and baked it.

QUESTION

A schoolteacher writes "King Henry died by drinking chocolate milk" on a whiteboard. Why?

CLUES

- They're not teaching history.
- This phrase can help prevent confusion.
- "By" represents the word "Base."
- It's a mnemonic for something.
- It's a sequence that's useful in math.

SOLUTION

It's a mnemonic for the decimal value places.

NOTES

They are a math teacher. The first letters of each word correspond with the prefixes for decimal place values, from kilo- (for 1,000) to milli- (for 1/1000).

- King = kilo- (×1,000)
- Henry = hecta- (×100)
- Died = deca- (×10)
- By = base unit (×1)
- Drinking = deci- (×1/10)
- Chocolate = centi- (×1/100)
- Milk = milli- (×1/1000)

■ ■ ■

Another useful mathematical mnemonic is "**I V**alue **X**ylophones **L**ike **C**ows **D**ig **M**ilk," for the Roman numerals from 1 to 1,000.

The Fibonacci numbers are 0, 1, 1, 2, 3, 5, 8, 13, 21, 34, 55, 89... where each number is formed by adding the previous two. Named after the 13th-century mathematician Leonardo of Pisa (aka Leonardo Fibonacci), the sequence can be seen in nature, such as the seed patterns of a sunflower and the number of spirals on a pinecone or pineapple. After a few terms, the sequence is also a mnemonic for converting from miles to kilometers by taking the next number in the sequence; for example, 34 miles per hour is roughly 55 kilometers per hour.

The phrases "Apple Pie Are Square" and "Cherry Pie Delicious" are two mnemonics used to help recall the formulas for the area and circumference of a circle: $A = \pi r^2$ [pi × (radius squared)], and $C = \pi d$ [pi × diameter].

TOM—STUMPED I knew it was a mnemonic from the first question, but I absolutely could not work out the sequence. And on "Base," I thought it was chemistry!

QUESTION

The *New York Times* printed its usual crossword on November 5, 1996—an election day. The clue for 39 & 43 Across was "The headline of tomorrow's newspaper." The printed solution the next day was "CLINTON ELECTED." How were they seemingly so sure of the election's outcome?

CLUES

- The crossword constructor hadn't been given an inside tip on the likely result.
- What were the circumstances of the 1996 election?
- The name of Clinton's opponent had a useful feature.
- What might have happened if the Republican leader had won?
- Clinton's opponent was Bob Dole.

SOLUTION

They weren't—the grid also worked if Bob Dole had won.

NOTES

The grid was devised so that it worked regardless of whether CLINTON ELECTED or BOB DOLE ELECTED was entered in the 14 squares.

What was most remarkable was that all the Down clues that intersected the letters CLINTON and BOB DOLE had to be written in such a way that they also had two possible correct answers. For example, there was "Black Halloween animal" (CAT or BAT), "Sewing shop purchase" (YARN or YARD), and "Trumpet" (BOAST or BLAST).

■ ■ ■

While word squares have been known since antiquity, the first recognizable modern crossword puzzle was printed in the *New York World* newspaper in 1913. Its creator, English journalist Arthur Wynne, called it a "word-cross puzzle."

In 1924, inspired by his puzzle-mad Aunt Wixie, publisher Dick Simon and his business partner Max Schuster enjoyed huge success with the first *Cross Word Puzzle Book* and its sequels. A pencil was attached to each copy to make it as simple as possible to get addicted. The puzzles became such a huge fad that crossword-themed dresses and jewelry were created. Libraries had to ration the use of dictionaries for those looking for an elusive word.

Ironically, the *New York Times* wasn't initially that impressed with the crossword puzzle, with a 1924 editorial dismissing them as "a primitive form of mental exercise." They held off publishing their own puzzle until 1942.

TOM—0 Clues This one I knew; I've seen that crossword before.

Scan to see both versions of the solved crossword.

QUESTION

In *The Lord of the Flies* by William Golding, the gang of boys on a faraway island start a fire. What's the problem with this scene?

BEST OF

CLUES

- They use a particular item from one of the other characters.
- The boy concerned is called Piggy, who has a particular character trait.
- Piggy is extremely nearsighted.
- What item did they borrow from Piggy to start the fire?
- What is it about the item that means physics works against them?

SOLUTION

The lenses in Piggy's eyeglasses are the wrong type to start a fire.

NOTES

Piggy was nearsighted, so he would need strong, diverging lenses. That is the type that pushes light beams farther apart, and so can't focus light.

Even if Piggy were farsighted, most converging lenses found in standard eyeglasses aren't usually powerful enough to start a fire. However, by putting a drop of water in the middle of the lens, you can bend the light further and it becomes easier to set something alight.

■ ■ ■

"Lens" comes from the Latin word for "lentil," because the classic shape for a convex lens strongly resembles a lentil.

The design for the Fresnel lens—made from concentric glass rings—was completed by Frenchman Augustin-Jean Fresnel in 1822. Developed for use in lighthouses, it concentrates the light into a strong, steady beam in a particular direction.

The anomalocaris (meaning "weird shrimp") was an ancient three-foot-long crustacean from around 500 million years ago. By analyzing a pair of eyes found in shale deposits, researchers estimate that the creature had 30,000 lenses per eye. If that seems far-fetched, some species of dragonfly alive today have 28,000 lenses per eye.

Bifocal lenses—which allow the user to see both near and far—were invented by Benjamin Franklin in 1785. He simply sliced two different sets of lenses horizontally and mounted them back into an eyeglass frame, one half on top of the other.

QUESTION

Out of over 270 stations on the London Underground network, only a handful—such as Brixton, Walthamstow, and Heathrow Terminal 5—are missing something familiar. What is missing, and why?

CLUES

- The three stations listed are on the outer part of the network.
- In fact, they are all at the end of the line.
- However, not all end-of-the-line stations are missing these.
- These things are seen at platform level.
- Millions of people notice these on the Underground each year.

SOLUTION

a. Advertisements on the wall opposite the platform.
b. Because there's nearly always a train waiting at the platform.

Question submitted by Harry G

NOTES

The stations listed are both underground and at the end of a "line." When the train arrives to let people off, it stays there and waits for some minutes to let people board for the journey back. This blocks the view of the wall where the advertising hoardings would be and, besides, arriving passengers are able to walk straight onto the train anyway.

At other "end-of-the-line" stations, the circumstances might be different. Some stations, for instance, have a choice of destination. As such, there's still a reason to have something for waiting passengers to look at.

■ ■ ■

A form of billboard can be traced back to the Egyptians. Tall stone obelisks were erected to communicate new laws and treaties to the people. In Roman times, advertisements consisted of graffiti that was painted or etched on walls, and public announcements were written on whitewashed wooden boards called alba (hence the word "album").

The music and entertainment magazine *Billboard* began in 1894 as a trade magazine for the bill-posting and advertising sector. As new forms of entertainment were invented, it widened its coverage over the years to include mechanical amusement machines, films, and jukeboxes. It began publishing its first music charts in the 1930s.

TOM—4 Clues I've been to most of those stations, and somehow I'd never noticed the lack of advertisements on those platforms. I suppose that's the point!

QUESTION

In China, why are large, rectangular pieces of cardboard given to people dressed as bears and pandas, among other costumes?

BEST OF

CLUES

- They're not professional actors and aren't doing this for entertainment.
- The people are fulfilling a legal obligation.
- They're also trying to keep something a secret, for good reason.
- The rectangular pieces of cardboard are something you'd be delighted to receive.
- This happens for promotional purposes.

SOLUTION

They're lottery winners, trying to protect their identity while collecting their prize money.

NOTES

While gambling is largely forbidden in China, the government's two state lotteries (the Welfare Lottery and the Sports Lottery) are exempt. It's an official rule that lottery winners must collect their prize in person and take part in publicity.

Some winners keep their newfound fortune secret from their families. One man was concerned that his son would "not work or study hard in future" if he knew that his dad had won a fortune. Other costumes used include Baymax from *Big Hero 6*, Mickey Mouse, and some of the Transformers.

■ ■ ■

In the UK, 10,000 people a week play the numbers 1, 2, 3, 4, 5, 6 in the main Lotto draw. In 1995, an amazing 133 people won its jackpot, largely because the winning numbers came from the same two columns on the paper entry form; people had lazily ticked the same pattern of numbers with their pencil.

The world's largest lottery is the Spanish Christmas Lottery, with over €2.5 billion in total sales. Schoolchildren sing the winning numbers chosen from 100,000 wooden balls. In 2023, the top prize (El Gordo—"the fat one") had a prize pool of €740 million, divided among as many as 185 winning tickets, each earning €4 million. Ticket prices are high, so each ticket is divided into ten "decimos" costing €20 and potentially winning €400,000.

The Great Wall of China and Queen Elizabeth I's war with Spain were paid for by lotteries. Claude Monet was called up for military service in Algiers by lottery, and US troops were selected for the Vietnam War by having their birthdays drawn at random on television.

QUESTION

Opened in 1966, One Wilshire in downtown Los Angeles was once an unassuming, 30-story office building. Then, after two decades of upturn, it was bought in 2013 for $437 million—nearly triple the price for equivalent business space in L.A. Why?

CLUES

- The height of the building was helpful to its business.
- The timings listed are important.
- The business benefited from being in downtown L.A.
- Its location turned out to be rather unique.
- What type of modern business boomed in the early 1990s?

SOLUTION

It became the West Coast hub for internet traffic.

Question submitted by Owen Busler

NOTES

The building was situated near AT&T's switching station, which provided direct internet connection to undersea data cables. It also helped that they were able to put a microwave dish on the tall building's roof.

After a 1992 renovation, the building attracted more telecom companies as tenants. This synergy was accelerated by providing a room where the tenants could interconnect their systems if they wanted to do so.

In 2015, it was one of the three most-connected points on the internet (the other two being in New York and London). It's believed that one-third of all US-to-Asia internet traffic passes through this building.

■ ■ ■

Approximately 99 percent of all international internet traffic goes through underwater cables. They are not a new idea. In 1858, the first transatlantic telegraph cable was able to send messages between Newfoundland and Ireland.

Modern transatlantic fiber-optic cables can transmit information at 99.7 percent of the speed of light. They are laid at depths of up to 26,000 feet (8,000 meters), the equivalent of Mount Everest's height. Cables at shallower depths are buried under the seafloor to protect them from inquisitive sharks, anchors, and fishing fleets. If a cable is damaged, ships equipped with robots or special grappling irons can raise each end to the surface so that it can be repaired.

TOM—5 Clues I had no idea until the final clue, despite working with internet stuff for a lot of my life.

QUESTION

BEST OF

An advertisement featuring a famous painting was placed next to an elevator in an ingenious position. The ad's tag line reads "Be born again." Who will you become, if just for a moment?

CLUES

- The painting had to be placed very precisely.
- Part of the painting necessarily had to come out of the frame for this effect to work.
- The painting is a famous work from the Renaissance period.
- What pose might you be in when calling an elevator?
- The real painting can be found in the Sistine Chapel.

SOLUTION

You will feel like Adam, touching fingers with God.

NOTES

Michelangelo's *Creation of Adam* is depicted to the right-hand side of the elevator. When someone wants to press the button for the elevator, it appears as if they are touching God's finger. The ad was for a plastic surgeon.

In the painting, God gives life to Adam as they almost touch fingertips. It is one detail from the series of frescoes from the Book of Genesis, painted on the ceiling of the Sistine Chapel, Vatican City, from 1508 to 1512.

■ ■ ■

Michelangelo wrote a poem about painting the Sistine Chapel vault, saying: "My stomach's squashed under my chin, my beard's pointing at heaven, my brain's crushed in a casket, my breast twists like a harpy's."

When Clement VII began to punish republican sympathizers, Michelangelo hid in a secret room in the basement of the Medici Chapel of the Basilica di San Lorenzo. He stayed there for three months, sketching on the walls to keep himself occupied. The secret room and its graffiti weren't discovered until 1975.

Michelangelo's sculpture of David was carved from a single block of marble called "The Giant." The 40-year-old stone, quarried for the cathedral in Florence, had been rejected by at least one other sculptor.

Michelangelo was involved in an attempted art fraud. Early in his career, he was commissioned to carve a long-lost statue of a cupid, which was going to be miraculously "discovered" in the ground and sold to Cardinal Riario. The scam was uncovered, and the money refunded.

Scan to see the advertisement.

QUESTION

In Lee Child's debut novel, *The Killing Floor*, a counterfeiting gang exploits a vulnerability that particularly affects US dollars. It allows fake notes to avoid detection by UV pen. What is it?

CLUES

- Printing is not necessarily the hardest part of counterfeiting.
- This is not a feature that most other countries suffer from.
- This feature causes issues for the visually impaired.
- If the UV pen indicates the note is real, what does that mean?
- Other than the appearance, how else do you judge whether a note is genuine?

SOLUTION

All US denominations are printed on the same-sized paper.

NOTES

One of the hardest parts of counterfeiting is obtaining a paper that has the right look and feel. US dollar notes are printed on a material made from 75 percent cotton, 25 percent linen.

Unusually, each denomination of note is printed on the same size of paper. Therefore, it is possible to obtain $1 bills, bleach the ink, and try to reprint them with a higher face value.

Although anti-counterfeiting techniques have improved, this method can still defeat simple detection methods, such as a UV pen, since the paper is "genuine." In 2022, it was reported that Hollis Forteau of New Jersey had likely printed $235,000 worth of $100 bills on bleached notes before he and his conspirators were caught.

■ ■ ■

The paper for US banknotes has been supplied by Crane and Co. since 1879. It takes 4,000 folds—backward and forward—before the note splits in two.

The US dollar is the world's most popular reserve currency. It's believed that—in terms of total value—more than half of all US currency is in circulation outside of the US itself. Independent countries that use the US dollar as an official currency include Ecuador, El Salvador, Zimbabwe, Palau, and Panama.

One theory for the origin of the dollar symbol is that it came from the Spanish peso, which was written as "PS" in the late 18th century. The two letters were sometimes written on top of each other, and it became "$" over time.

As a sign of confidence to his financial backers, Philo Farnsworth used a dollar sign on the screen when demonstrating his pioneering television system to the press in 1928.

TOM—4 Clues There really ought to be more accessibility on US bills: bright colors, different sizes, large numbers, and tactile markings are all really useful!

QUESTION

In the 1930s, the burger chain White Castle hit upon a way to make their stores virtually immune to large rent increases. What was it?

BEST OF

CLUES

- The same technique also allowed them to respond to venues that had poor sales.
- To achieve this, they set up a subsidiary called the Porcelain Steel Buildings Company.
- White Castle restaurants were made with a very forward-thinking construction method.
- The restaurants were typically very small.
- If you don't like where you are, what's the easiest way to go somewhere else?

SOLUTION

Their "prefab" restaurants were small enough to be loaded on a truck and moved elsewhere.

NOTES

If a location wasn't performing well, or the landlord of the current location was threatening to jack up the rent, they could put the entire building onto a truck and move it somewhere better. This was relatively easy to do because they were compact and prefabricated.

Early White Castle restaurants looked like an archetypal castle, with turrets and crenelated ramparts. The design was modeled after Chicago's Water Tower.

■ ■ ■

Prefabricating buildings, or "modular construction," was used by the ancient Romans. Forts for the city wall were put together by dovetailing several wall pieces. The larger forts housed 20 men and had most of the amenities of a standard barracks, including gates, kitchens, latrines, and running water.

Modern prefabrication techniques are rapidly increasing the possible rate of construction. In 2015, an entire 57-story skyscraper sprouted up in just 19 days. The Mini Sky City tower in Changsha, China, is a mixed-use building with 215,000 square yards (180,000 square meters) of floor space.

The Eiffel Tower was built in "only" two years because two-thirds of the 2,500,000 rivets were already inserted at the factory using steam hammers. The entire thing was put together as a giant jigsaw of over 18,000 parts, each 5.5 yards (5 meters) long on average.

Founded in 1912, Huf Haus GmbH is a famous German company that manufactures prefab buildings with timber frames and sheet glass frontages. Each one is made individually to order.

QUESTION

Adam was able to enjoy his Thanksgiving dinner a little more because Eve wasn't afraid of spiders. Why?

CLUES

- Adam and Eve haven't met.
- What traditional foods are served at Thanksgiving?
- Thankfully, Eve also didn't have aquaphobia.
- This concerns something that is an accompaniment.
- Eve works in the agriculture industry.

LEVEL 4: MAIN QUESTIONS

SOLUTION

Farmers use (wolf) spiders to protect cranberry vines.

NOTES

Cranberry vines are attacked by various pests. Spiders are beneficial because they eat a wide variety of prey, including aphids, caterpillars, and flies. Wolf spiders grow in larger numbers in a small area and can eliminate huge quantities of insects.

The fruits are hollow, so farmers flood the vines at harvest time to let the berries float. If any spiders end up in the water, they will climb on the tallest thing they can see—which is often the people collecting the berries.

■ ■ ■

Cranberries are not really berries, but "epigynous fruits" or "false berries," a status they share with bananas, coffee, and blueberries. They were originally called crane berries because the pink flowers on the vines reminded people of the head of a crane, the large wading bird.

Native Americans used cranberries with dried deer meat to make pemmican, a high-calorie food that was useful in survival situations. They also used the fruit in poultices when trying to extract poison from arrow wounds.

The Guinness World Records credits André Ortolf with the record for "Fastest time to eat 500 grams of cranberry sauce." His time of 42.94 seconds was set in 2016.

The Irish rock band The Cranberries were originally called The Cranberry Saw Us (a childish pun on "cranberry sauce"), but the new name stuck when a demo tape was sent back, addressed to "The Cranberries."

TOM—3 Clues I once got an invitation to film a video in a cranberry bog, and I'm now quite happy that it didn't work out.

QUESTION

Jasper visits his friend Chloe. He picks up a deck of playing cards, saying "I see your family are fans of games." When Chloe replies, "Yes, we like to play . . ." Jasper interrupts with "Euchre, isn't it?" How could he tell?

CLUES

- There was nothing obvious lying around (e.g., a book on euchre).
- They liked to play euchre a lot.
- The deck was the only clue he needed.
- Not all card games are played the same way.
- It was a visual clue.

SOLUTION

Only about half of the cards in the deck were worn out.

NOTES

When Jasper picked up the deck, he saw that only 24 cards were worn, while the others looked nearly new. The 24 cards are the 9, 10, jack, queen, king, and ace of each suit. (There are other variations that use the 8 and 7 also.)

Euchre is the only common card game that uses that set of 24 cards from a standard deck. Piquet is similar, using 24 cards from a selection of 32.

■ ■ ■

If a similar deck was found, they could have been playing pinochle—a game that uses two copies of a similar 9-to-ace deck, making 48 cards in total. The rules of euchre require a highest-possible trump card, which evolved into the joker that we know today.

The modern pack of 52 playing cards comes from the Minor Arcana of the tarot deck. A superfluous knight card was removed, and the wands, swords, cups, and pentacles (or coins) suits were replaced by clubs, spades, hearts, and diamonds, respectively.

The king used to be the highest-ranked card in a suit, but it was replaced by the ace during the French Revolution as a symbolic gesture of the "little guy" getting one up on royalty.

Playing cards were taxed in the UK from 1588 to 1960. Card manufacturers would buy pre-marked ace of spades cards from the government's stamp office to indicate that the duty had been paid. This card is also nicknamed the Advertising Card because manufacturers often feature their company name or logo on it.

TOM—5 Clues This was a guess. I had no idea that there were common games that didn't include all 52 cards.

QUESTION

Occasionally, the legendary Munich nightclub P1 has held a "pinkelparty" called Einhalten. The drinks are free from opening time until . . . when?

CLUES

- It's not a fixed time.
- There are several word-based clues in the question.
- This situation is beneficial to the clubbers, and amuses the (rather sadistic) nightclub owners.
- This scheme causes the most amount of discomfort for early attendees.
- The more they could endure, the better value people received.

SOLUTION

Someone has to use the toilet.

NOTES

Einhalten means "retain." The clubbers must hold in their bladders for as long as possible.

The party starts at 9 p.m., with the toilets locked and security guards minding the doors. They only open the doors once someone demands to be let in. At that point, the drinks are no longer free. After their visit, the "spoilsport" has to go up to the center stage to be briefly pilloried in medieval-style stocks. The toilets are then available for everyone to use.

■ ■ ■

Pinkelparty ("pee party") is the German word for a boozy celebration when the father's friends metaphorically "wet the baby's head." It takes place sometime between the birth and the baptism, and is sometimes signified by hanging a bedsheet or flag out of a window.

When the building was previously occupied by US forces for use as an officers' club in 1949, visitors had difficulty pronouncing the address "Prinzregentenstraße 1," so they called it P1 instead. P1 is known for being a celebrity hotspot, especially for the players of FC Bayern Munich. Whitney Houston, Robert De Niro, and Mick Jagger have all patronized the club.

P1 has an infamously strict door policy. When a famous rock band was refused entry to the nightclub without a prior invite—saying, "But we are the Scorpions"—the bouncer simply replied, "Exactly."

TOM—4 Clues This seems like a terrible idea for so many reasons. I didn't have any idea about this until near the end, and even then I really wasn't sure.

QUESTION

Michelle Knapp bought a secondhand car for $300. A few days later, after a 164-mph collision, she was able to sell the damaged car for $25,000 . . . and make an additional $50,000 on top of that. How?

BEST OF

CLUES

- She was at home when the collision happened.
- The collision wasn't between two cars.
- Her car wasn't even moving at the time of the collision.
- The car didn't collide with another car—but another thing.
- The other thing was worth $50,000 at the time.

SOLUTION

Her car was hit by a meteorite.

NOTES

In 1992, a 27-pound meteorite fell in Peekskill, New York, breaking through the rear corner of her car. Both the damaged Chevy Malibu and the meteorite itself were sold for large sums to interested collectors.

Because many people were recording their local football games on a Friday night, the meteorite was caught on video at 16 different locations. Today, specimens of the meteorite sell for around $150 per gram.

■ ■ ■

To clear up the terminology, meteoroids are rocks that are in space, whereas meteorites are fragments that hit the ground. If it burns up before reaching a planet's surface (i.e., a "shooting star"), it's a meteor.

Since over 40 tons of meteoroids fall toward Earth every day, shooting stars can be seen year-round. Periods when the sky is particularly active are called meteor showers; a famous example is the Perseids, where up to 200 meteors per hour can be seen. They are created by debris from the comet Swift-Tuttle, which peaks in mid-August.

Weighing 60 tons, the Hoba meteorite is the largest found to date, discovered on a Namibian farm in 1920. It remains where it fell as a national monument, although tourists taking chunks as "souvenirs" is a problem. In 2021, a large piece weighing 6.2 pounds (2.85 kilograms) that had been (ahem) "obtained" back in 1958 was sold by Bonhams auction house for $59,000.

If you Google the word "meteorite," you are treated to a short "shooting star" animation effect as an Easter egg.

QUESTION

The Janet Jackson song "Rhythm Nation" has been officially declared a cybersecurity vulnerability. When played, it can make some computers inoperable after a time, and even affect other computers nearby. How?

CLUES

- This tends to affect older computers.
- It affected a popular brand of a particular component.
- How could playing a file affect a nearby computer?
- It didn't harm newer computers with solid-state drives.
- It has to do with the properties of the sound.

SOLUTION

The song contained a resonant frequency that caused hard drives to crash.

Question submitted by Cheryl Dostaler

NOTES

In 2022, it was found that the music video for "Rhythm Nation" contained a frequency that was very similar to the natural resonant frequency of a popular model of Seagate hard drive.

Even playing the video in the vicinity of a vulnerable computer could cause device malfunctions and system crashes. An audio filter that blocked out the offending frequency was added in a later version.

■ ■ ■

One of the most famous and visual examples of resonance is the original Tacoma Narrows Bridge in the state of Washington. It opened in July 1940 as the third-longest suspension bridge in the world by main span, but quickly became known as "Galloping Gertie" due to its wild movements in windy conditions. Thankfully, no lives were lost when the bridge collapsed that November as it was closed to traffic at the time.

As their name implies, MRI (magnetic resonance imaging) machines use the resonant frequency of the hydrogen atom to create detailed medical scans.

Male Bornean tree frogs try to increase their chances of attracting females by choosing a water-filled hole in a tree for their mating call. They try several different "test tones" to match the resonant frequency of this specific tree hole so that their mating call sounds as impressive as possible.

TOM—0 Clues This one I knew—it's not just that I saw the news story, it's that many people sent it over to me, knowing it's the sort of thing I might be interested in. (They were right!)

QUESTION

Why was Saint Lucia the first team to enter the stadium in the Parade of Nations during the 2004 Olympic Games?

- -

CLUES

- By tradition, the Greek team usually enters first—but not this time.
- The second and third teams were St. Vincent and the Grenadines, and San Marino.
- This sequence was different from the ordering used in most other years.
- What traditionally dictates the order in which the teams enter?
- Where were the 2004 Olympics held?

LEVEL 4: MAIN QUESTIONS

SOLUTION

Because "Saint Lucia" comes alphabetically first in Greek.

NOTES

The first team in the Parade of Nations is usually Greece, to honor their tradition of founding the ancient Olympics. However, because the 2004 Olympics were held in their home country in Athens, they went last instead.

The other teams were introduced in strict alphabetical order in the host's language, Greek. The first teams were:

- Αγία Λουκία (Saint Lucia)
- Αγιος Βικέντιος και Γρεναδίνες (St. Vincent and the Grenadines)
- Αγιος Μαρίνος (San Marino)

■ ■ ■

For the 2008 games in Beijing, the teams were introduced according to the number (and then the order) of the strokes in the first character of the country's name in Mandarin.

With a population of around 11,000, Nauru is the smallest nation by headcount to compete in the Olympics. Competing in athletics, weightlifting, and judo, their athletes have yet to medal—a status shared by over 60 other countries or territories.

Other countries that often appear at a different point in the Parade of Nations than where you might expect (even using English names) include:

- North Korea: under "D" for "Democratic People's Republic of Korea"
- Macedonia: under "F" for "Former Yugoslav Republic of Macedonia"
- Ivory Coast: under "C" for its French name, "Côte d'Ivoire"

TOM—1 Clue I knew it had to be an alphabetical order question, but it took me a while to work out which alphabet.

QUESTION

Claire entered a busy arcade and noticed that it had her favorite pinball machine. Even from halfway across the room, she could tell that the machine was probably broken, although there was seemingly nothing amiss. How?

CLUES

- To a novice, the game would seem undamaged upon visual inspection.
- If Claire played the game, her suspicions would have been proven correct.
- She was able to notice something without even looking at the main playfield.
- What other visual clue could she see easily from "halfway across the room"?
- What things appear on a pinball machine's display?

SOLUTION

The "replay score" advertised by the LED display was much lower than she would expect.

NOTES

Each time a player scores well, the machine's algorithm hikes up the score that is required for a "replay" (a free game). The very low replay score likely indicated that there was a broken flipper or similar mechanical flaw that made scoring difficult.

■ ■ ■

Pinball machines are modern developments from the French game of bagatelle, where a ball bearing navigates a field of pins and hurdles to fall into scoring holes. The plunger that launches the ball into play remains a feature of many modern machines.

If you perform an unusual move on a pinball machine and hear "moo" or see a cow in the graphics, you've unlocked a "hidden cow." They are the pinball industry's equivalent of an "Easter egg"; they caught on when a cow-mad pinball designer started to include them in his machines as an inside joke. Some machines have a secret "Midnight Madness" mode if you're playing late into the night.

New York City banned pinball machines in the early 1940s; Mayor Fiorello La Guardia (after whom the airport is named) regarded them as a form of gambling. The ban was overturned in 1976, when expert player Roger Sharpe demonstrated to Manhattan City Council that pinball was a game of skill, not luck.

The best-selling pinball machine of all time was "The Addams Family," based on the 1991 film. Featuring new audio clips from Anjelica Huston and Raúl Juliá, the critically acclaimed machine shipped over 20,000 units.

TOM—STUMPED No idea! Pinball isn't something I know enough about, so I thought it might be some other aspect of the playfield. It makes sense that the replay score would adapt, though.

Acknowledgments

Tom and David would like to thank the following for their work on this book and the *Lateral with Tom Scott* podcast generally:

Our UK book editor, the irrepressible Ause Abdelhaq, and the team at Pan Macmillan. Their enthusiasm for the project has been second-to-none.

Francis Heaney and the team at Puzzlewright Press for their diligent and good-humored work on bringing this US edition to fruition.

Ben Clark at the Soho Agency, for his sage advice and expert handling from beginning to end.

Carina Rizvi, also at the Soho Agency, for administering the show's advertising and managing Tom generally.

Chris Hanel at Support Class, assisted by Dillon Pentz, for designing our graphical look for *Lateral*.

Evan Scow at Dava Marketing for his amazing thumbnails that adorn the audio podcast and video highlights.

Jacob Star at Caption+ for the best captions in the business.

Karl-Ola Kjellholm, whose music we use on the podcast.

Matt Mahon and Alan Bennett at The Podcast Studios, Dublin, for their studio services and expert know-how.

Extra special thanks to Julie Hassett, our amazing podcast & video editor, who nailed the style we wanted from the very beginning. Her technical skill, comic timing, and editorial nous has saved us countless hours. She's most definitely the Third Musketeer of the team.

All our lovely guests who kindly gave up their precious time to be so interesting and entertaining. During the first 30 episodes covered by this book, these were: Ali Spagnola, Amelie Brodeur, Becky Smethurst, Becky Stern, Bill Sunderland, Brady Haran, Brian McManus, Cleo Abram, Corry Will, Dani Siller, Devin Stone, Emily Yarid, Eric Johnson, Grady Hillhouse, Hayley Loren, Jabrils, Jade Tan-Holmes, Jason Slaughter, Jay Foreman,

Jordan Harrod, Karen Kavett, Kip Heath, Luke Cutforth, Mark Rober, Marques Brownlee, Mary Spender, Matt Parker, Mehdi Sadaghdar, Melissa Fernandes, Nahre Sol, Nicholas J. Johnson, Rowan Ellis, Sabrina Cruz, Saf AhmedMia, Sarah Renae Clark, Simone Giertz, Stuart Ashen, Taha Khan, Trace Dominguez, Vanessa Hill, Virginia Schutte, William Osman, Wren Weichman, Xyla Foxlin.

And finally, thank you to everyone who took the time to submit a question idea. We only get the opportunity to use a few of the submissions we receive, but appreciate everything that's sent in. We couldn't have made it this far without your help.

About the Authors

Tom Scott is a presenter and broadcaster with over six million subscribers on his YouTube channel. His videos have covered science, technology, and interesting curiosities in the world: everything from robotic warehouses to zero-gravity flights to remote outposts in the Arctic.

He has been in an airplane that sets off fireworks attached to it, passed out in a centrifuge, and abseiled off a wind turbine. More than 60 million viewers watched him send garlic bread to the edge of space... and then eat it when it landed.

Tom studied linguistics at York University, hosted *Gadget Geeks* for Sky One, and once had to run for Parliament dressed as a pirate after losing a bet.

David Bodycombe is an entertainment producer and writer who started contributing games to the original version of the action-adventure game show *The Crystal Maze* as a young viewer. He is now a full-time format consultant, content producer, and deviser of questions, puzzles, and games.

He was the original question editor of the BBC's lateral-thinking quiz show *Only Connect*, and worked on numerous other popular shows including *Treasure Hunt*, *The Krypton Factor*, *Armchair Detectives*, and Amazon's *007: Road to a Million*.

David's output has covered TV, radio, print, advertising, board games, live events, escape rooms, and now, podcasts. He studied mathematics at Durham University and is a two-time winner of the World Creative Thinking Championships.